I0117829

Mending Broken Hearts

Mending Broken Hearts

A Therapist's Guide to Post-Infidelity Repair

Tanya Schecter

IGUANA

Copyright © 2025 Tanya Schecter
Published by Iguana Books
720 Bathurst Street
Toronto, ON M5S 2R4

All rights reserved. No part of this publication may be reproduced, stored
in a retrieval system or transmitted, in any form or by any means,
electronic, mechanical, recording or otherwise (except brief passages for
purposes of review) without the prior permission of the author.

Publisher: Cheryl Hawley
Editor: Amanda Feeney
Front cover design: Jennifer Papineau

ISBN 978-1-77180-717-3 (paperback)
ISBN 978-1-77180-718-0 (epub)

This is an original print edition of *Mending Broken Hearts*.

To Olivier and Josh, my husband and son, and my family, all of whom have taught me much about how to live relationally. You have my heart forever.

Table of Contents

"The chains of matrimony are so heavy, it takes two to carry them, sometimes three."

—Alexandre Dumas

Chapter 1

Introduction

"How could you?" she cries in anguish.

"But it was only once. It didn't mean anything," he replies contritely, believing what he says, not truly understanding why she is so upset.

"I'll never be able to trust you again," she hiccups and begins to sob uncontrollably.

"What can I do to make it up to you? I'll do anything," he proclaims abjectly.

"Nothing! There's nothing you can do. You're a cheater, and a cheater never changes. I can't trust you anymore. You've ruined all our lives!" she rages.

"I may have cheated, but you're one cold fish," he retaliates.

Imagine that you are the therapist, and this isn't the first time you're seeing this couple, but the 20th. They're deeply locked in a negative spiral, and you can't see an end in sight. You're feeling increasingly uncomfortable, knowing that you should be able to help them move out of their cycle of blame, shame, recriminations, and rage, but you lack the skills to do so.

As this couple's therapist, you feel paralyzed, caught between wanting to help them and wanting to refer them to someone you're sure is more qualified. You may think that you're the only therapist who feels this way, but you're not alone. Couples counseling skills, never mind how to treat the specific issue of infidelity, are often only lightly touched on in graduate school, if at all. As a result, many couples therapists (especially those new to the field) are caught in this very quagmire when faced with a couple navigating their post-infidelity reality.

Many heterosexual couples experience infidelity at some point in their relationship, and infidelity is one of the most difficult issues to treat in therapy. As a couples therapist, having a roadmap that helps you identify where your couple currently is in the repair process and where they need to go makes this process easier and more effective. Essentially, it allows you to calmly, clearly, and successfully guide your couple through the reparative process and reconnect. Understanding infidelity's root causes, knowing what your couple needs to address to repair their relational rupture, and using effective therapeutic approaches and interventions is an essential part of this.

Why Is Addressing Infidelity So Important for Your Clients' Long-Term Relationship Success?

Relationships matter! In fact, according to Harvard's seminal 8-decade longitudinal study, relationships negatively and positively impact our well-being, and people who are engaged in positive relationships and connected with family and community are happier, are healthier, and live longer than those who aren't. More specifically, people who are in warm, trusting, satisfying, stable, and committed relationships are healthier, live longer, and experience a measure of protection against life's numerous physical and emotional challenges. As George Vaillant, who led the study from 1972 to 2004, has pointed out, relationships are our primary basis for healthy aging.

However, over time, our ideas about our relationship's role in our lives have changed dramatically, and this has impacted our ability to have these types of fulfilling and protective relationships. In previous decades, we had strong family connections that spanned multiple generations and strong relationships with other people in our communities. These bonds allowed multiple positive relationships to flourish, each potentially satisfying our unique relational needs, and enabled us to thrive.

Our current hyperconnected world stands in sharp contrast to this. Although we can reach anyone at a moment's notice by tapping on our phones or connecting "live" through video or phone, we feel less connected, more distracted, and less engaged in meaningful one-on-one interactions. As a result, social isolation (lack of proximity to others) and loneliness (perceived lack of connection with others) are on the rise.

As Esther Perel — a maven couples therapist who is known for her frank discussions about sex, intimacy, fidelity, and the changing nature of marriage — has pointed out, adding to this sense of alienation is the fact that while we used to look to our mates to mainly provide us with stability and security, we now look to them to provide us with everything we used to receive from our entire social network (i.e., connection, meaning, and purpose). We do this, all while expecting them to meet our sexual and emotional needs.

For most of us, this change has largely taken place without awareness, and we frequently take our underlying assumptions about committed relationships for granted: We don't talk about them with our partners or with others. In fact, our relational assumptions are often only challenged when their reality fails to live up to our expectations. This becomes apparent when we look at the issue of infidelity in committed heterosexual relationships.

"Till death do us part" reflects the commonly held assumption that marriage is both monogamous and for life. No matter what. This same assumption often holds true for those in committed relationships not formalized by marriage.

Despite this dominant narrative, 20% to 25% of married heterosexuals have engaged in extramarital sex in their current relationship, and 70% of all people, married or not, report having been unfaithful at some point in their lives. What stands out is that more than 90% of married heterosexuals subscribe to the belief that monogamy is critical for relationship survival and success, yet more than half of them admit to having been unfaithful at some point in time. So how do we reconcile this discrepancy?

Perel points out that this discrepancy is not a new one, noting that while infidelity has been condemned throughout the ages, it's almost universally practiced. North American numbers support this statement: 25% of marriages experience infidelity, and the number of women engaging in infidelity is on the rise. These startling figures indicate that our actual behavior lies in sharp contrast to our professed beliefs. Given these astonishing numbers, it's reasonable to assume that infidelity is the issue most likely to affect heterosexual couples over the course of their relationships.

What Is Infidelity Exactly?

Defining infidelity is hard because our perception of it is subjective and variable. However, according to Terry Real, the founder of Relational Life Therapy (RLT), all infidelity can be easily identified by 1) a transgression that breaks a relationship's contract, 2) a secret, and 3) involvement with a third party outside the relationship. Identifying a transgression isn't always easily accomplished since most heterosexual couples don't have an explicit contract that addresses infidelity. Instead, they rely on a vague one (i.e., we'll be faithful to one another).

Compounding the problem is the fact that each partner often has a very different idea of what fidelity means. These differences run the gamut from defining infidelity as sexual involvement of any kind with a third party to using pornography, turning elsewhere to satisfy emotional needs, desiring someone else even if the desire isn't acted upon, sharing personal information with a third party, and more. Each partner may also be inconsistent in their definition of infidelity, changing it over time. What's more, partners may fail to have open conversation about the issue. All of this contributes to each partner's uncertainty about where the line of transgression lies.

Secrecy is often an indicator that the involved partner knows they've engaged in an act that's crossed the line of transgression, if not for themselves, then for their partner. When the infidelity is discovered, this discrepancy is highlighted, and the line of transgression becomes defined for each partner. At this point, relational rupture typically occurs, the relationship is thrown into chaos, and partners question all previously held assumptions about their relationship's meaning and its future.

What's Possible for a Couple Post-Infidelity?

Almost always, when partners think about their post-infidelity reality, their decision about how they should proceed is informed by their beliefs and judgments surrounding the meaning of staying in their relationship or leaving it. The following commonly uttered statements about infidelity illustrate how much these beliefs and judgments can vary:

- "Cheating is just wrong. One strike and you're out."
- "No matter what, we'd always find a way to work it out."
- "I wouldn't stay with someone who cheated on me. Once a cheater, always a cheater."
- "My marriage is great, except for our sex life. Having an affair is what makes it possible for me to stay married."
- "I'd never be able to trust someone if I found out they cheated on me."
- "We don't talk about it, but we're both involved with other people."
- "I can't leave; we have three kids to raise."

As Perel has explored in her writings and much-viewed TED Talks, the stigma associated with different courses of action further complicates a couple's decision around how they should proceed post-infidelity. Specifically, while post-infidelity divorce used to be stigmatized (especially for women who left their marriages), the rise of feminism and women's rights has caused the stigma to shift to the partner who decides to stay in their marriage or relationship once infidelity has occurred and been exposed. This change in discourse can have an impact on a couple's post-infidelity relational trajectory and often contributes to their relationship's unpleasant demise.

Given that partners often have widely differing ideas about how to proceed post-infidelity, it's unsurprising that infidelity in a committed couple almost always causes a relational rupture. However, infidelity doesn't always mean that the relationship ends. In fact, many couples stay together and try to move past the transgression.

Perel likes to point out that even though more couples opt to stay together post-infidelity, it doesn't mean that they live happily ever after. Instead, she explains, a couple is likely to fall into one of three camps. The first type of couple never moves beyond animosity towards one another. Each partner recycles the same grievances, plays the blame game as if on lather, rinse, repeat, and holds the other person responsible for their misery. The second type of couple stays together out of a desire to honor their lifetime marriage vows, a desire to maintain their family and social circle, and/or a desire to adhere to their religious beliefs. These couples may return to a peaceful version of their marriage as it existed prior to the transgression, but their relationship doesn't fundamentally change. The third type of couple experiences the infidelity as a catalyst for change and transformation. Once they move beyond the infidelity, they, and their relationship, undergo a transformation and are changed for the better.

What Therapeutic Approaches Can You Use to Help Couples Positively Transform Their Relationships Post-Infidelity?

Interestingly, Esther Perel isn't the only therapist, and hers isn't the only therapeutic approach, to state that infidelity can act as a transformative catalyst for a couple, allowing them to rise like a phoenix from the ashes of their ruptured relationship to create a newer, stronger relationship, one that's rooted in deeper bonds based on transparency and true intimacy. Relational Life Therapy (RLT), Emotionally Focused Therapy (EFT), Psychobiological Approach to Couples Therapy (PACT), and Gottman all promote the idea that if a couple addresses the underlying issues that provoked the infidelity and reestablish trust, their relationship can not only survive but thrive.

Each of these established approaches to couples therapy focuses on repairing the relational rupture and reestablishing trust as a foundational element of the couple's ongoing success. Of these approaches, only RLT has a clear methodology for accomplishing this and for helping the couple transform their relationship into a more relational entity.

Unlike the other previously mentioned approaches, RLT's focus and end goal is for a couple to emerge from the infidelity not only operating more relationally, but also transformed by it. Its three-phased approach for dealing with infidelity is solidly grounded in its theoretical underpinnings and is designed to achieve this outcome. Adopting this approach can help you be more skilled and adept at helping couples not only stay together, but also achieve post-infidelity relational transformation.

What's the Purpose of This Book?

The purpose of this book is twofold. The first is to provide you with a greater understanding of the issues at play when infidelity occurs. The second is to provide a therapeutic methodology you can apply to help your clients 1) repair relational rupture after their experience with infidelity, and 2) use the experience of infidelity as a catalyst to rebirth their relationship and, in doing so, transform it into something that's more sustainable, intimate, and life-enhancing.

Specifically, this book will explore the following topics:

- Why couples engage in infidelity

- Issues a couple needs to address to repair a relational rupture caused by infidelity

- RLT's theoretical approach

- RLT's approach to treating infidelity

- How you can use the Connected Hearts Inspire (CHI) Relationship Map and its tools to guide couples through the RLT process of repairing and healing from infidelity

How Can This Book Help You Become a Better Therapist?

Since infidelity is a ubiquitous issue in couples therapy, you'll likely be confronted with it at some point in your career. Helping your clients successfully navigate infidelity is easier if you understand the underlying contributing factors along with what's required to help couples (and individuals) recover and move past it. More specifically, having a framework and tools to help your clients move forward increases their odds of coming out on the other side of infidelity as a unified, functional, and thriving whole.

Because these tools are rarely taught in depth in graduate school and each therapeutic approach typically requires that you engage in extensive and costly skills training, you're unlikely to master the requisite skills until you're well into your career. Whether you're a novice or a seasoned therapist, this book provides synthesized information related to infidelity (causes and impacts), an overview of a relationship-based approach to treating infidelity, and explanations of how to use a relationship map and other interventions to support this process. Ultimately, applying this information when treating couples who are suffering from infidelity can help you save relationships that might otherwise be unnecessary casualties.

Why Did I Decide to Write This Book and What Are My Underpinning Beliefs?

I'm a cisgender woman who was previously divorced and is currently married. While infidelity hasn't touched me directly in my romantic relationships, almost everyone I know has either been unfaithful or experienced a partner who was unfaithful at some point in time. From personal second-hand experience, I'm aware of the devastation that this issue can wreak upon a committed relationship and the people involved and of the very hard work needed for the relationship to survive. I'm also aware that too few manage to move from simple survival to transformative revival.

As a therapist, I'm also aware of how easy it is to have a knee-jerk reaction to tales of infidelity and get stuck in the notion that each story has a clear victim and villain. Knowing that the issue is more nuanced, I'm also aware that a couple's successful post-infidelity outcome resulting from therapeutic assistance is dependent on the therapist not falling into this trap of black-and-white thinking and on being able to keep an open mind as to what's possible.

I believe that relational transformation resulting from infidelity is possible and that infidelity is often a symptom of larger problems belonging to one or more people and/or the system in which they operate. I believe these issues need to be resolved for fundamental change to take place and that this requires all partners to commit to listening to one another, to owning their contribution to the problem(s), and to engaging in the painstaking process of changing their patterns and ways of interacting with one another.

I also believe that while we're all part of a system in which we both act and are acted upon, we're ultimately the authors of our own stories, able to envision and bring to life the outcomes we desire. However, to do so, we need more than just a script: We need the appropriate tools.

These two beliefs profoundly impact how I show up as a therapist. I'm a staunch advocate for 1) understanding the environment in which we exist, including the hidden forces that influence us and the invisible impacts our actions have in creating our current reality, and 2) providing clients with new tools while expanding their emotional and interpersonal capacities so they can create the outcomes they yearn for.

It's my hope that this book will help new and future therapists do the same for couples who are doggedly plagued by infidelity's often long-felt reverberations. I also hope this book will be useful to existing clinicians who are helping couples to move through infidelity's morass.

A Word About the Case Studies Included in This Book

I've included case studies throughout this book to provide a sense of the painful and often contradictory messages that emerge in the therapy room when treating infidelity. While the content is real, the case studies are amalgamations of real clients designed to provide you with in-depth and realistic examples of the concepts discussed while protecting clients' identities and privacy.

In the second half of this book, you'll meet "Emelia" and "Bob" through their own words. While Emelia and Bob's stories are true, they are composite creations. Their larger story is designed to illustrate the complexity that underlies relational repair and transformation while protecting identities.

Definitions of Terms Used in This Book

The following terms are used throughout this book. For easy reference, you can also find a copy of these terms and definitions in the Glossary of Terms at the end of this book.

Adaptive child: According to RLT, the adaptive child is the part of each person that was forged after the age of five due to relational trauma. The adaptive child is a child's version of an adult and tends to think in black-and-white terms and be perfectionistic, relentless, rigid, harsh, certain, and hard, while living in a body that is tight/tense.

Attachment style: The bonding pattern that children learn and bring, as adults, into their relationships.

Betrayal: A violation of a person's trust, confidence, expectation, agreement, or moral standard.

Blatant: An RLT term that refers to the relational partner who's more relationally dysfunctional and who frequently engages in boundary-violating and grandiose behaviors.

Characterological change: A change in a person's fundamental character.

Circle of health: An RLT term that refers to the place where someone operates as a wise adult and doesn't escape into shame or grandiosity, seeing themselves as equal to (not better or less than) the person with whom they are interacting.

First consciousness: An RLT term that refers to the knee jerk reaction a person has to their partner when they're operating out of their limbic system. It is typically associated with a fight, flight, freeze, or fawn response.

Grandiosity: A person's sense of entitlement that's frequently expressed in boundary-violating behaviors (e.g., yelling, controlling, retaliation), with little regard for the impact of their behavior on others.

Hurt partner: The person in the relationship who's betrayed and hurt by the infidelity.

Involved partner: The partner in the relationship who's committing infidelity.

Joining through the truth: An RLT term that refers to confronting a client with the truth about their bad behavior in such a way that they feel seen and understood.

Latent: An RLT term that refers to the partner with the least amount of power in the relationship.

Leverage: A partner's motivation for change.

Losing relational strategies: Relational strategies that, when employed, undermine intimacy and/or the relationship itself. According to RLT, there are five losing relational strategies: withdrawal, needing to be right, control, retaliation, and unbridled self-expression.

Psychological patriarchy: The belief that 1) humans can be divided into two halves based on masculine and feminine qualities, and 2) feminine qualities are worth less than masculine qualities (i.e., masculine qualities are typically exalted by the larger society).

Second consciousness: An RLT term that refers to a person who is operating out of their wise adult and who has access to their prefrontal cortex. This state is marked by an ability to self-regulate and interact in a relational manner.

Shame: A person's belief that they, as a person, are not good or worthy (i.e., there is something wrong with them at their core).

Stance-stance-dance: An RLT term used to reflect a relational dance that's composed of the relational stances adopted by each partner.

Transmission reception work: An RLT term that refers to work that's done with the latent so that they can receive the new, more relational behaviors that the blatant is engaging in.

Wise adult: An RLT term that refers to a person who can pause and refrain from using losing relational strategies when confronted or engaged in conflict and, instead, respond intentionally. Wise adults typically operate out of their prefrontal cortex and are defined by being nuanced, realistic, forgiving, flexible, warm, yielding, humble, and relaxed in their body.

How Is This Book Organized?

Chapter two first defines what infidelity is and the forms it can take. The chapter then reviews the different factors that can contribute to infidelity.

Chapter three provides an in-depth exploration of the issues a couple needs to address for relational repair to occur.

Chapter four explains Relational Life Therapy (RLT) — its history, theory of change, and approach — as well as RLT's beliefs about the therapist's role.

Chapter five explores how you can work with couples to use infidelity as a source of relational transformation. Specifically, it explains how to apply RLT's approach to infidelity to engender post-infidelity relational transformation. Understanding what to do, when, and why, provides you with a concrete roadmap you can consult to facilitate healing, repair, and transformation.

Chapter six explores RLT's strengths and limitations in its approach to post-infidelity repair and relational healing. As a therapist, being aware of RLT's strengths and limitations allows you to keep an open mind as to when and where you might want to supplement your approach with alternative techniques and tools to create a more robust therapeutic experience.

Chapter seven explains the CHI Relationship Map and its therapeutic interventions. In this chapter, you'll learn how to use the

CHI Map to 1) help partners identify when they're moving farther apart from one another, and 2) create the boundaries required to contain them when this happens. You'll also learn how to use conflict resolution tools embedded within the CHI Map as an adjunct to RLT's approach to treating infidelity.

Chapter eight focuses on key skills you can utilize to keep you, and your clients, centered, grounded, and focused as you guide your couple through the repair process to evoke a more positive, relational outcome.

At the end of each chapter, you'll find a section labeled TL;DR (Too Long; Didn't Read). This section contains a summary of the chapter's key points in a concise format that you can readily reference.

"It takes two to tango but just one dance with the devil to bring the house down."

—Jason Versey

Chapter 2

Infidelity and Relational Rupture

The story of infidelity is as old as the written word and runs consistently throughout the ages. Only the individual story details differ. Think of King David who committed infidelity with Bathsheba; King Henry VIII who committed infidelity in most, if not all, of his marriages; Simone de Beauvoir who repeatedly escaped her relationship with Sartre via clandestine rendezvous with underage women; and Bill Clinton who famously diddled Monica Lewinsky.

In the Judeo-Christian tradition, infidelity lies at the core of humanity's written story. As presented in the Old Testament, when morality was first formalized on Mount Sinai, infidelity was seen as such a taboo and associated with so many negative impacts that it was given its own commandment, "Thou shalt not commit adultery." This commandment is based on the idea that fidelity is a foundation of a solid marital bond, essential for establishing intimacy and maintaining a sacred covenant.

Although this belief forms the basis for much of the Western world's relationships, not all Western cultures rooted in this belief see infidelity as the same destructive force to the institution of marriage or to a relationship's underpinning fabric. The French, for example, have traditionally had affairs and romantic dalliances without treating them as a fundamental threat to their primary relationships or as a reflection of problems that exist within them. In fact, in this culture, discovery of infidelity by one partner does not always lead to relational rupture or to relational dissolution.

Other cultures not rooted in the Judeo-Christian tradition also see infidelity as problematic and as an impediment to marital longevity. Islam, for example, strongly condemns infidelity and, in its extreme, condones the stoning to death of women who engage in it.

Given these differing understandings of infidelity's importance, its meaning, and the potential negative consequences associated with it, the question remains as to why a partner might decide to engage in it. This question is even more pertinent when partners believe that monogamy is key to their relationship's long-term success and to their ongoing intimacy with one another.

Intimacy in a romantic relationship, however, often develops alongside unaddressed or unacknowledged issues. These issues may contribute to partners turning towards infidelity to solve their unhappiness or a perceived lack in their relationship. This is true even for those in happy marriages. To understand what leads a couple into infidelity's imbroglio, we need to understand the various forms that infidelity can take, along with contributing factors. This chapter will first explore how infidelity is defined and then look at factors that contribute to its occurrence.

Infidelity Defined

Three Common Elements

While people may define infidelity differently, Terry Real provides clear criteria for evaluating whether infidelity has occurred. According to him, all infidelity contains three elements: Secrecy, the first element, can occur by omission or commission. A transgression, the second element, is an act that violates a couple's established relational ground rules. The third element involves one partner turning towards a third party that lies outside of the primary relationship for gratification. This party can be a person, object (e.g., phone, blow-up doll), or activity (e.g., video games, tennis). Infidelity exists when all three elements are present.

Although it's easy to think that infidelity only occurs in a monogamous relationship, it's important to remember that infidelity can just as easily occur in committed non-monogamous relationships since it's the elements of secrecy, a transgression, and the involvement of a party outside of the primary relationship that define it. Because of this, identifying infidelity isn't always so clear cut for all involved. Consider the following example.

Sarah, Sam, and Mike are in a committed polyamorous relationship. They've all agreed that it's okay for each of them to spend time with others outside their primary relationship as long as the other relationship partners are introduced to the person beforehand, and each feels assured that the outsider will abide by their established safety rules around sex.

Recently, Mike started spending a significant amount of one-on-one time with Cindy, a co-worker, without letting Sarah and Sam know. When Sarah found out and told Sam, both were upset and felt that Mike had betrayed their agreement. When confronted, Mike felt unjustly accused since he wasn't yet involved with Cindy sexually. He believed that he had not transgressed the relationship's rules.

Regardless, Sarah and Sam were upset, as they felt that Mike had indeed contravened one of the agreements that bound them as a throuple. As a result, tension in their relationship started to escalate. Eventually, all three attended therapy to work through the incident and reestablish clear boundaries.

Sexual and Emotional Infidelity

Infidelity typically involves a third party with whom one partner engages to satisfy their unmet romantic, emotional, or sexual needs and desires. Infidelity can be sexual or emotional, and these types of infidelity can occur independently or be intertwined.

Sexual Infidelity

Sexual infidelity involves engaging in sexual behaviors, with another person or oneself (e.g., watching pornography), and may or may not involve intercourse. Activities involved in this category are wide ranging (e.g., intercourse, anal sex, oral sex, kissing, masturbating, looking at someone who's undressed).

Emotional Infidelity

Emotional infidelity involves a person spending time with a person or object other than their partner. Emotional infidelity is associated with the emotions of love and betrayal and may or may not lead to sexual infidelity. Due to its amorphous nature, this type of infidelity may be harder to recognize. Consider the following example.

Mattie had always enjoyed a warm and collegial friendship with Nigel, her business partner. For years, Mattie and Bruce, her husband, had socialized with Nigel and his wife, often celebrating milestones, such as birthdays, and holidays together.

Over the past few months, however, Bruce had been preoccupied with a large legal case he was overseeing at his firm. With Bruce frequently unavailable, Mattie found herself turning to Nigel not only to bounce business ideas off of, but also to share her thoughts, feelings, and emotions, ones she had traditionally only shared with Bruce. Nigel, in turn, found himself reciprocating.

It didn't take very long before Mattie found herself not only turning towards Nigel before turning towards Bruce to share what was going on in her life and in her heart, but also thinking about him, and not Bruce, as her best friend. Although Mattie still loved Bruce and never wanted to leave him, she was also finding it hard to identify who she wanted to prioritize in her life and where her primary allegiances lay.

Differing Perspectives

Whether infidelity is sexual or emotional, the involved partner and the hurt partner may not experience it as equally grievous. This, in and of itself, may cause a rupture. Consider the following example.

Jake recently discovered that his wife, Tiffany, had been secretly texting an ex-boyfriend. He feels that Tiffany has been unfaithful even though she never met the ex-boyfriend in person or discussed anything sexual.

Tiffany feels she did nothing wrong. She believes that texting her ex-boyfriend is the same as texting her girlfriends, which she does frequently.

Jake and Tiffany both agree that Tiffany was acting in secrecy, even if by omission rather than intent. However, only Jake feels that their relational boundary was transgressed. Left unaddressed, feelings of betrayal and mistrust may take root on Jake's side; feelings that may have long-lasting implications for their relationship.

What Influences Someone to Engage in Infidelity?

While it's easy to descend into ideas of villain and victim and into judgments about a philanderer's moral bankruptcy, the reality of why someone might engage in infidelity is nuanced and complex. Infidelity is usually a symptom of an existing relational problem, not its root cause. Consequently, when someone engages in infidelity, one or more of the following factors is likely at play.

Lack of Intimacy and Dissatisfaction

Expectations

As previously discussed, Esther Perel has pointed out that in previous generations, people mainly looked to marriage as a vehicle for survival, procreation, or financial gain. Today, most Westerners look at marriage solely as a means of expressing their love for their partner. This is equally true for those in long-term committed relationships.

At the same time, whereas we historically looked to many people to fulfill our needs (i.e., the "it takes a village" approach), we now expect our partner to fulfill most, if not all, of them. We expect our partners to provide love, companionship, support, and intellectual stimulation and be our overall go-to person.

This is a lot to expect from our romantic relationships, and it places a huge amount of pressure on each partner. Consequently, when a partner's emotional and/or physical needs aren't being met within their primary relationship, they may choose to engage in emotional or physical acts with a third (or more) party to try and get them satisfied.

Dissatisfaction

A partner who's generally dissatisfied with their relationship's intimacy level or with a specific aspect of their relationship (emotional, sexual, or intellectual) may be propelled to look elsewhere for satisfaction. In fact, lack of emotional and/or physical intimacy is a factor that frequently prods someone into unfaithfulness. For many, intimacy problems are a primary source of relational dissatisfaction, and they provide the rationale for a large percentage of infidelity-related activities.

Gender Impact

In Western society, there's a well-entrenched belief that men more frequently engage in sexual infidelity and women more frequently engage in emotional infidelity. However, a recent study indicates that this isn't true. Both men and women report engaging in infidelity-related behavior as a means of seeking the affection, understanding, and attention that's missing in their primary relationship. Consider the following example.

Kayla loved her husband Alex but was tired of being rebuffed each time she tried to share her feelings with him. After ten years of asking Alex to pay attention to her at the end of the day and doing whatever she could think of to engage him sexually, she was feeling increasingly lonely, invisible, and rejected.

Exasperated, she joined a running group to try and release her hurt and frustration through exercise. There, she started talking to John, a co-runner, who was smart, funny, engaged, and always complimentary. While she initially looked forward to seeing him on Saturday morning runs, knowing they'd be exchanging small talk, she soon found herself meeting John at the local coffee shop so they could talk more in depth about their lives. As their intimacy grew, things progressed. Soon, Kayla was in a full-blown intimate relationship with John and confronting a decision as to what she should do about her marriage.

Sexual Desire Discrepancy

Almost 80% of couples experience a discrepancy in sexual desire. This is defined as one partner desiring sex more frequently than the other. A difference in sexual interests or kinks can also be an aspect of desire discrepancy. If left unmanaged, desire discrepancy can strain a relationship and may lead to infidelity.

Men, as compared to women, tend to be more liberal in terms of seeing infidelity as an acceptable means of satisfying their sexual needs. It's unclear, however, whether this belief impacts their behavior vis-à-vis engaging in infidelity. Ultimately, both men and women turn to thirds to satisfy unmet sexual desires. This can be very nuanced, as illustrated by the following case.

Sally met Steve when she was in her mid-30s and he was in his mid-40s. They immediately hit it off, realizing they had a lot in common: they both placed a high value on family and wanted to start one as quickly as possible; they both came from a similar religious background and were equally involved with their churches; they had similar values and goals regarding finances; and they both enjoyed many of the same activities, including travel, tennis, and hikes in the countryside. Before they knew it, they had tied the knot, and their first baby was on the way.

Although Sally realized early on that she was more sexually adventurous than Steve, and that he was happy with a more "vanilla" sex life, she decided that, on balance, this was something she could adapt to and work with, given that everything else in their relationship more than met her needs. She also thought she'd be able to bring Steve around — if not fully into her realm of sexual kink, at least by moving the needle a little. However, after a decade of marriage, two kids, and years spent trying to cajole Steve into trying something outside of his sexual comfort zone, Sally realized her current status quo was as good as it was going to get.

Sally soon found herself spending some of her nights in online chat groups, talking with others in her situation about how to get her needs met. It wasn't long before she found herself going out in the evenings to join members from her groups and making up excuses to Steve to cover where she was going. Although she felt bad about lying to Steve, Sally told herself that engaging in these activities was a way to ensure their marriage stayed intact.

Poor Impulse Control

Desires are defined as an impulse to increase pleasure, alleviate discomfort, or fulfill a specific want. Although everyone has sexual and emotional desires, not everyone acts on them. In fact, many people in committed relationships who experience desire for others don't act on it.

This restraint may be due to a fear of rejection, wanting to honor their commitments to their partner, wanting to respect their own values, or fear of being shunned if found out. Conversely, people with low levels of self-control and/or poor self-regulation may be more likely to act on sexual or romantic desires and, thus, may be more likely to engage in infidelity.

Attachment Style

Attachment style, based on John Bowlby's work, is defined as the bonding pattern that children learn and bring, as adults, into their relationships. Bowlby identified four attachment styles:

1)   Secure attachment

2)   Insecure-ambivalent or anxious attachment

3)   Insecure-avoidant attachment

4)   Disorganized attachment

A person's attachment style often influences the degree to which they're likely to engage in infidelity.

Secure Attachment

A person who has a secure attachment style had a caregiver who consistently responded to their needs and consistently provided them with comfort and reassurance when things went wrong. This helped them develop trust in their caregiver and in the relationship.

According to Stan Tatkin, the founder of the PACT approach to couples therapy, people with a secure attachment style tend to protect their relationship from thirds (i.e., any person or activity that threatens their partner or relationship). They're likely to not only be concerned with maintaining their partner's happiness, but to also focus on maintaining their relationship's equilibrium. Consequently, they're the least likely to engage in infidelity.

Insecure-Ambivalent/Anxious Attachment

A person who has an insecure-ambivalent or anxious attachment style had a caregiver who was inconsistent in terms of responding to their needs. This created a lack of trust in the caregiver and in the relationship.

In keeping with Stan Tatkin's analysis, people who have an insecure-ambivalent or anxious attachment style may engage in infidelity as a preemptive strike against the rejection they perceive as inevitable. Additionally, because they require external regulation when distressed, they experience a partner who's unresponsive or unavailable as threatening. As a result, their threat response may activate their partner's threat response, creating an escalating pattern of non-responsiveness and antagonism. Since someone with an insecure-ambivalent or anxious attachment style requires connection for self-regulation, they may seek a third party to fulfill this need.

Insecure-Avoidant Attachment

A person who has an insecure-avoidant attachment style had a caregiver who was insensitive when responding to their needs. As a result, they learned not to count on the relationship or on their caregiver when in distress. Typically, not only do they believe that self-reliance is the only way they can get their needs met, they also experience intimate personal relationships as threatening. For them, distancing themselves provides relief.

Stan Tatkin explains that people with an insecure-avoidant attachment style are at greatest risk of their partner engaging in infidelity because they tend to experience intimate personal relationships as threatening. As their threat response is activated, their sexual desires reduce, and they're often left disgusted and turned off by their partner's bids for intimacy. This can manifest in sexual dysfunction or distancing. The avoidant's partner may not understand what's triggering this reaction and may look for relief from a third party.

Disorganized Attachment

A person with a disorganized attachment style had a caregiver who was inconsistent when responding to their needs and often acted in an atypical manner (e.g., abusing, rejecting, or manipulating). These people have an unpredictable approach-avoid style of relating to any attachments. There's no clear research indicating how this attachment style impacts the frequency of infidelity.

Revenge and Retaliation

Belinda Berman-Real, a certified sexual addictions therapist, defines retaliation as a perverse form of communication in which the hurt partner tries to inflict the same level of hurt that they've experienced on the offending partner. Their goal is to make their partner understand the negative impact they've incurred and, ideally, feel remorse.

Some people engage in infidelity as an act of revenge or retaliation. A person with one or more of the following traits is more likely to be unfaithful to exact revenge or retaliation on their previously straying partner.

Low Empathy

Someone low in empathy is less likely to forgive their unfaithful partner, even if the infidelity is over, and they themselves may engage in infidelity as an act of revenge. The following is an example of how this can unfold.

When Jeremy found out that Micayla had been unfaithful, he was extremely angry. Although Micayla repeatedly apologized to Jeremy for her actions, often groveling for his forgiveness while promising to adhere to all his rules and to never engage in infidelity again, Jeremy couldn't move past the infidelity. He ruminated on it and sank into his anger, something that ultimately became part of their relationship's fabric.

Micayla eventually convinced Jeremy to go to couples therapy. After a year and a half, things started to improve with Micayla noticing that Jeremy didn't seem as angry and bitter about her prior involvement. She assumed therapy was working and that they were making headway on the issues that had contributed to her looking outside their relationship for fulfillment in the first place. Some sessions later, however, it emerged that Jeremy himself had recently engaged in infidelity, something that was now over.

Micayla was devastated to learn about Jeremy's infidelity and to understand that Jeremy's anger had lessened not because things had changed between them, but because he felt like the score was now even. At this point, their relationship's needle moved back into the negative with all their original issues back on the table.

Psychopathy

Engaging in revenge activities can cause a person to feel guilt, risk their personal safety or that of their partner, and potentially expose them to reputational loss. People with a high level of psychopathy are likely to underestimate their behaviors' negative impacts and overestimate their positive impacts. They also have higher levels of impulsivity and risk-taking behavior. Consequently, they may engage in infidelity as an act of revenge, regardless of perceived risk level.

Narcissism

People with narcissistic tendencies are typically low on empathy, highly invested in protecting their reputation, and likely to engage in retaliation or revenge. This is even more true when dealing with infidelity since narcissistic people have low levels of self-esteem and are highly motivated to outperform perceived competitors.

Opportunity

Instead of being a premeditated activity, people are sometimes prompted to engage in infidelity because of situational factors or opportunity (e.g., traveling to a new area where they are unknown). In fact, in one study, up to 70% of respondents cited situational factors as their primary reason for engaging in infidelity, although this was truer for men than women. Work and the internet are two of the most prominent birthplaces of opportunistic infidelity.

Work

The past fifty years have heralded a large shift in the division of labor. Increasingly, more and more women work outside their homes in paid positions. There, they, along with men, spend time talking with others about topics that mutually interest them. They also work, sometimes physically and/or intellectually closely, with others who share their interests. These relationships occasionally develop, extending beyond the workplace, which creates opportunities for intimacy and infidelity. A person who has a job involving regular travel, frequent exposure to trauma, long hours, or being in an unhealthy or toxic work environment is also more likely to engage in infidelity. Consider the following example.

Alicia married young, at the age of twenty, and was a stay-at-home mother until her children entered high school. At that point, she started working in a shipping company. At first, she had an entry-level job. Being a hard worker, she quickly worked her way up the corporate ladder, eventually becoming a human resource director.

Over time, as she developed relationships with the company's stakeholders and clients around the world, travel was required. Initially, she limited her travel, fitting it in between school holidays. As her children graduated and left home, and as she rose higher in the company, her job became more demanding in terms of travel. She was frequently away for weeks at a time, often accompanied by Nick, her right-hand man. The more time they spent together away from home, the closer they became.

At the same time, Alicia began to feel estranged from Jared, her husband of twenty years. With the children gone and little in common in terms of careers, she noticed that the silences between them grew as her excitement at seeing him at the end of her work trips dwindled.

Before she knew it, she and Nick were having a secretive relationship, one that was largely eclipsing her marriage.

Internet

Over recent decades, the internet's ubiquity has created a unique opportunity for both sexes to engage in infidelity, whether they leave their home or not. In fact, almost 30% of people go online to pursue sexual gratification either through porn sites or by engaging (live or virtually) with a real person. Newer technologies, such as virtual reality porn and teledildonics, which allows someone to experience physical tactile sensations, make this even more compelling.

Of this 30%, almost two-thirds participate in offline sexual activities with their online sexual partners. Dedicated sites for infidelity, such as AshleyMadison.com, make this even easier. With the tag line "Life is short. Have an affair," the website, in existence since 2002, claims to facilitate one million affairs each month and, as of 2019, purported to have a membership of over 60 million.

Gender and Cultural Norms Concerning Sexuality

Different cultures have different norms concerning infidelity. Cultures also differ in their perception about and definitions of infidelity. A recent study, for example, indicated that men and women living in cultures where fathers are more invested and involved in childcare tend to see infidelity in a more negative light. However, more research is needed in this area.

Different racial and gender groups within the dominant culture may also have differing norms or attitudes. This, in turn, may influence infidelity rates. In North America, for example, 22% of Black, 16% of White, and 13% of Hispanic people reported being unfaithful to their spouse. When these stats were further broken down by gender, infidelity rates for men increased: 28% of Black men, 20% of White men, and 16% of Hispanic men reported being unfaithful.

Religion, Education, Income, Commitment, and Family History

Religion

People who are non-religious are more likely to engage in infidelity. Being a member of a close-knit religious community may act as a deterrent since the person may adhere to religious values that condemn the practice (e.g., commandment seven: thou shalt not commit adultery), or they may fear being shunned, shamed, or at odds with the community and relationships on which they rely for connection and validation if their infidelity were discovered. Consider the following example.

Naomi had been unhappy in her marriage ever since her children were born. She and her husband, Noam, had little in common beyond their children and their joint goal of retaining their home, something that swallowed most of their combined income and energy.

Although Naomi fantasized about having an affair, even going so far as to explore different ways that she could do so, her fear of being found out prevented her from following through. While her commitment to her Jewish faith provided somewhat of a deterrent, it was the thought of being found out and exposed to her larger community that was the real prevention. Ultimately, Naomi was worried about being negatively judged and losing not only the close relationships that she relied on, but also her overall social standing in the community, something she was well aware would also impact her children.

Education and Income

People with higher levels of education and/or higher incomes are more apt to engage in infidelity. Influencing factors may include a wider social network, a greater ability to travel, a greater ability to afford potential costs associated with infidelity (e.g., meals, hotels, vacations), greater work flexibility, a greater ability to pay for childcare and leave the house, etc.

Interestingly, a couple is more likely to experience infidelity when one spouse depends on the other economically. This is truer for couples aged 18–32 when the man is financially dependent on the woman. Essentially, economic parity acts as a guardrail against infidelity.

Commitment and Family History

Married couples are at greater risk of experiencing infidelity if they cohabitated before getting married or a commitment to uphold their marriage vows isn't a central precept of their marriage. A couple is also at greater risk of infidelity when one partner's commitment to making the marriage work is low. This is because the person with low commitment may not take a long view of their relationship or see value in working through periods of dissatisfaction. Similarly, people who grew up in families in which infidelity was present are more likely to engage in it themselves. Consider the following example.

Barney and Puneet lived together for four years before getting married. Although he was 42 and she was 38, it was the first time each of them had lived with another person with whom they were in an intimate and committed relationship. Wanting to start a family, they decided to tie the knot, and Puneet become pregnant within the year.

By the time the baby was born, Barney was feeling frustrated with Puneet and with the way his career and their life were unfolding. Outwardly, he appeared to be agreeable, going along with what Puneet wanted. But in reality, he was growing more and more disconnected from her, often agreeing with her more out of apathy than conviction.

Having grown up in a family where emotions weren't talked about and conflict was brushed under the rug, Barney didn't know how to address any of the discomfort he was experiencing. His fear of upsetting Puneet and of her emotional backlash furthered his desire to maintain distance. Given that his own parents had had an open marriage, eventually replacing each other with newer models who appeared more desirable, it's not surprising that Barney soon found himself involved with another woman who appeared to be attentive to his needs and emotionally stroke him where it itched.

By the time he and Puneet went to couples therapy, he had little desire to invest the time and effort that would be required to repair their relationship. His marriage was over soon after.

It was only years later, once the affair had ended and he'd undergone intensive therapy, that he realized his model of a committed relationship was flawed. As he put it, "Had I only realized that relationships aren't expendable, and that they require work, I might have put more effort into trying to fix my marriage."

Presence of Children

A couple's children may act as a deterrent to infidelity. This is especially true if a person values having their children grow up in a home where both parents are present and the marriage is intact. Paradoxically, children may create competing demands on a couple's relationship. This may foster conditions in which one or both partners' needs are not met and cause them to start looking elsewhere for fulfillment.

Summary

As a therapist, you can help your couple navigate their post-infidelity relationship and help them move through the resulting turmoil by making it easier for them to explore the issues that contributed to the infidelity. Because infidelity doesn't develop in a vacuum, a person's unmet needs, their history with (and perceptions about) relationships, their psychological makeup, their attachment style, familial history, gender, culture, religion, and values all impact their choice to engage (or not to engage) in acts of infidelity. Layered on top of this, opportunities for infidelity created by modern-day living can add a further crimp to understanding the situation.

While it might appear easier for your couple to cut their losses and leave their relationship post-infidelity, the likelihood that one or all partners will find themselves in another relationship where infidelity occurs is high. Helping your couple explore their differences in perceptions about what constitutes infidelity and their lack of clear communication about the subject alleviates the murkiness around the issue, increases intimacy, and fosters potential for your couple to move through the transgression and survive as a unified whole.

Specifically, engaging in this process helps your couple establish clear boundaries around their relationship, ones that involve an explicit definition of the relationship's ground rules and what constitutes a transgression. This creates a more solid foundation from which they can move forward.

TL;DR

Infidelity Defined

- Infidelity is defined by the presence of **three elements**: 1) secrecy, 2) a transgression of the relationship's boundaries or ground rules, and 3) one person turning to a third party (person, object, or activity) that lies outside the primary relationship.

- Infidelity can occur in **any committed relationship**, including non-monogamous ones.

- Infidelity can be **sexual and emotional**. These can occur independently or simultaneously.

- Infidelity can occur in **happy marriages**.

Factors Influencing Engagement in Infidelity

- One partner's **dissatisfaction** with their level of emotional or physical intimacy can lead to infidelity.

- Unmanaged **sexual desire discrepancy** (either one partner desiring sex more frequently than the other or differences in sexual interests or kinks), in particular, can strain a relationship and lead to infidelity.

- A partner with **poor impulse control** is at higher risk of engaging in infidelity.

- **Attachment style** has a large impact on how a relationship unfolds. People with a **secure** attachment style are more likely to safeguard their relationship against thirds and focus on maintaining their relationship's equilibrium. People with an

insecure-ambivalent/anxious attachment style are more likely to engage in infidelity as a preemptive strike against the rejection they perceive as inevitable. People with an **insecure-avoidant** attachment style are more likely to experience infidelity from a partner whom they have distanced themselves from.

- People **low in empathy, high in psychopathy, and/or high in narcissistic traits** are more likely to engage in infidelity as a form of retaliation and revenge.

- **Opportunity** arising from work or situational factors may promote infidelity. Although more men than women engage in infidelity for these reasons, the numbers are evening out.

- The **internet** provides men and women with easy access and many opportunities to engage in infidelity, alone or with others. Almost 30% of people who engage in infidelity online also participate in real-life sexual activities with their online sexual partners.

- **Gender** and **cultural norms** can impact rates of infidelity in differing ways.

- People who are **non-religious** and those who have **higher incomes** are more likely to engage in infidelity.

- Married couples who don't consider their **marriage vows** as central to their relationship are more likely to suffer from infidelity. **Cohabitating** before getting married, having one partner who has a low individual commitment to making the marriage work, or having one partner who grew up in a family where infidelity was present are risk factors for infidelity.

- **Children** can both mitigate against or be a risk factor for infidelity.

"We all make mistakes, but what matters is how we go back and fix them."

—Rwynn Christian

Chapter 3

Relational Repair

"I know it happened over two decades ago, but do you ever think about when he was involved with that other woman? Does it still impact you as a couple?" I gingerly asked a friend.

"Do I think about it?" she asked incredulously.

"I know we don't really talk about it, and we don't have to talk about it now if you don't want to," I said softly, trying to give her an out.

"Of course, I think about it," she exploded. "I think about it all the time and it's always there between us, even if it's just simmering in the background. It affects everything!"

"Oh?" I probed.

"I mean, we're great roommates and we get along for the most part, but I'm always thinking about it. I worry about what would happen if our kids found out. She wasn't much older than our youngest daughter is now. I worry about what they would think of him — and how they would judge me for staying with him afterwards. It's always there, influencing how much or how little I can trust him at any given time. I'll never trust him 100%. And, really, as much as I love him, I hate that he did this to us," she said with a resigned sigh.

Partners frequently suffer little and big betrayals throughout their relationship's lifespan. Typically, couples repeatedly recover from them. In fact, when a couple works through a major betrayal in a productive way, their relationship usually emerges stronger. Infidelity, however, holds a special place in the hall of betrayal.

For a committed couple, infidelity almost always causes a relational rupture, one that's difficult to recover from. But this doesn't always mean the relationship is over. In fact, according to the American Psychological Association, approximately 50% of people who were unfaithful in their relationship stay together. Moreover, men who were previously unfaithful are even more likely to stay married than women who were unfaithful.

A relationship can survive infidelity for a variety of reasons. A couple may decide to try and repair their relationship out of a desire to stay together, a desire to learn from the infidelity, or because the hurt partner either forgives the involved partner or decides to stay with them as an act of kindness. Alternatively, a couple may decide to stay together for financial reasons, to remain with their children full time, to keep their family intact, or to uphold their religious or spiritual beliefs and values.

If left untreated, infidelity's legacy (and its root causes) is likely to reemerge in unanticipated ways, creating ongoing and secondary levels of damage. Over time, this damage can slowly erode a couple's relational efficacy, despite both partners' good intentions. Consequently, if a couple decides to continue their relationship post-infidelity, they may attend therapy to help them heal their relational rupture and find a new equilibrium.

In the therapy, many (sometimes conflicting) emotions are present. As a therapist, you must attend to the emotions arising directly from the infidelity, along with the underlying issues, all while providing the couple with support and guidance. This chapter is dedicated to understanding what this might look like.

Emotional Distress

"I can't sleep. I can't eat. I feel like crap. I look like I've aged a hundred years. Every time I think I might be starting to feel okay, I'm hit with thoughts of Matt in bed with her, doing things to her that he never did to me! And then, I feel angry all over again. I can't help it. I don't want to feel this way. I want to be able to forgive him. But each time this happens, and I see his hangdog face in front of me, I just want to smack

him," Evie cries. *"Why? Why did Matt have to do this?"* she wails in anguish. *"I just wish we could go back to how we were before, when I loved him without reserve."*

Unfortunately, Evie's response to her partner's infidelity isn't unusual. Infidelity leaves a wake of emotional distress and trauma in its path. Depression, anxiety, extreme anger, feelings of betrayal, insecurity, rage, shame, guilt, jealousy, rejection, resentment, fear, and sadness are all common post-infidelity manifestations. In fact, a hurt partner may display symptoms akin to post-traumatic stress disorder, including hyperarousal, rumination, intrusive flashbacks, and emotional dissociation.

The hurt partner is distressed by the act of infidelity and by the fact that their assumptions about what they could count on in their relationship are shattered; the feelings of safety, surety, and fidelity that they assumed were unassailable are crushed. The involved partner is also often distressed. The roots of their distress lie in the harm they've caused to their partner and to their relationship. They may also feel shame about themself and their actions, fear about what the future holds, sadness, and regret.

Sometimes, the involved partner denies their infidelity or does a partial disclosure in a misguided attempt to alleviate their partner's immediate suffering and protect themself and/or their relationship. Typically, however, this increases one or both partners' distress. This, in turn, manifests itself as further depression, anxiety, post-traumatic stress, and a mistrust of others.

An involved partner who makes concessions towards their partner from the outset (e.g., is truthful about the details of the infidelity; provides their partner with reassurances about their present-day behaviors; provides their partner with ways of establishing their truthfulness, including tracking their location on their phone and providing them with access to their emails and social media accounts) has the largest positive impact on alleviating emotional distress. Similarly, couples who talk about their relationship post-infidelity and work through their issues tend to have less emotional distress.

Betrayal and Trust

"At first, I couldn't believe that Matt wasn't the guy I knew him to be. I couldn't believe he would betray our marriage vows, that he would betray me," Evie sniffles. "Now, even though he swears he's told me everything, even though he always answers his phone and tells me where he is whenever I call and check on him, even though he lets me look at his phone and his messages and has me hooked into his calendar, and even though he's apologized and sworn to me that he'll never do it again, a part of me doesn't trust him. I don't even know if I can trust that our marriage means what I once thought it does. I want to trust him, I just don't know if I can," she says mournfully.

As Terry Real succinctly puts it, after infidelity is discovered, the hurt partner wonders, "How could you do this to me?" and "How do I know you won't do it again?" In essence, the hurt partner's trust in the relationship and in their partner is shattered. This may be exacerbated if the involved partner has a history of lying and/or infidelity, or if the couple has previously experienced some other form of betrayal.

According to Terry Gaspard, a person's ability to heal from betrayal and recover trust after infidelity is vastly improved if the involved partner

- ends the infidelity;
- provides their partner with a full disclosure;
- demonstrates remorse;
- finds a way to atone for their infidelity;
- is willing to answer all questions and deal with all their partner's feelings; and
- promises not to repeat the infidelity.

The hurt partner's behavior also impacts the couple's healing process. The hurt partner can positively influence the healing process by

- using "I" statements in all communications;
- avoiding endless rehashing of the infidelity's details; and

- working towards acceptance and forgiveness.

Guilt and Shame

"I'm sorry, Evie. I know I'm a piece of crap. I ruined everything and I'm not worth you or our relationship. I know you're better than me and that I don't deserve you. I can't eat or sleep knowing what I did to you and the kids. I hate myself for who I've become — I think about how horrible I am all day long," Matt says when they first come in for therapy.

The involved partner may feel guilt and/or shame during and after the infidelity. A person who feels shame doesn't just feel bad about what they've done, they also feel badly about themselves as a person, as if something is fundamentally and irrevocably wrong with them. A person experiencing guilt, on the other hand, feels bad about a specific behavior or act they've committed, while still seeing themselves as a worthwhile (although flawed) human being.

As Terry Real explains, this distinction is important. A person who feels shame can't engage in the post-infidelity repair process because they typically feel so badly about themselves that they want to withdraw from the person they've hurt. Someone who feels guilt, on the other hand, is remorseful and can focus on the person they've hurt and attempt to repair the harm. In therapy, having the involved partner shift from shame to guilt is a pivotal element that allows the repair process to unfold.

In Evie and Matt's case, once Matt could see himself as a flawed human being who had engaged in an act that he regretted, rather than a person who was rotten at his core, he was able to fully focus on Evie, her pain, and what she needed to begin trusting him again. That's when their true healing began.

Anger, Resentment, and Communication Breakdown

Lehe and Doug had been together for eleven years, most of which were very happy. Early on in their relationship, Doug had taken a job in which he worked long hours away from home, often traveling with

Maggie, his immediate manager. Although Doug and Maggie were never romantically involved, Doug began turning towards Maggie to meet his emotional needs.

It started with Doug sharing his work-related worries with Maggie. Eventually, it shifted to him turning to Maggie to talk about his personal life. Soon after, Doug found himself thinking about Maggie when he was at home, often counting the hours until he could see her again. All this left Lehe feeling as if she was on the outside of their relationship, a third unwanted and undervalued wheel.

Once Doug realized that his friendship with Maggie was negatively impacting his relationship with Lehe, he put some distance between himself and Maggie. Shortly thereafter, he quit his job so that he wouldn't have to interact with her anymore.

Even though Doug was the one to end the relationship, Lehe couldn't get over what she saw as his emotional infidelity. It cast a specter over their relationship for almost a decade, often manifesting as Lehe feeling anxious when Doug was out of sight and jealous and fearful when he spent time with anyone other than her. This dynamic continued until they both went to therapy and processed their underlying issues, emotions, and lingering resentments about the infidelity.

Men and women tend to respond differently to different types of infidelity. Typically, men are more jealous over physical infidelity, whereas women are more upset about emotional infidelity. However, when confronted with sexual infidelity, both men and women express intense emotional reactions, especially anger. In contrast, emotional infidelity tends to mainly result in anxiety and jealousy.

As Leon Seltzer explains, regardless of the type of infidelity, moving through the resulting emotions so that both partners can engage effectively in the repair process requires that 1) the involved partner listen to their partner's feelings, and 2) the hurt partner, once heard, stop pummeling the involved partner with accusations and recriminations. Failing to do this can increase the involved partner's shame, induce anger, and inhibit their ability to be available for their partner. Ultimately, in this scenario, the hurt partner finds it harder to forgive. If communication breaks down with anger and resentment replacing remorse and empathy, the couple will likely create a self-perpetuating cycle of animosity, and true repair will never take place.

Differences in Perspectives

Because partners may differ in terms of their ideas about what constitutes infidelity, they may also disagree about whether the involved partner has actually engaged in infidelity (e.g., use of pornography or fantasizing about a co-worker). If the couple can't agree or the hurt party can't obtain acknowledgment that their partner has transgressed their relationship's ground rules, the repair process may stall. The repair process may also stall if only one of the partners believes that the infidelity can be overcome.

Summary

When discovered, infidelity causes a relational rupture. It often exposes previously invisible relational issues that clawed at the fabric knitting the couple together. Consequently, the post-infidelity repair process isn't an easy one for a couple to wade through. Emotions are high, and trust in the other person, and in the relationship itself, is at an all-time low.

As the therapist, by helping your couple work through the underlying issues that contributed to the infidelity, you play a key role in their post-infidelity repair process. Being effective at this requires that you help them address their underlying issues, all while helping them express their emotions in an appropriate manner. Doing this helps your couple move through the repair process and towards relational transformation.

TL;DR

- **Relational betrayals** (large and small) happen throughout a relationship's lifespan. Some betrayals may be addressed along the way, and some may be ongoing. Most, however, don't cause deep **relational ruptures**. In fact, if an issue is worked through, a couple typically emerges stronger for it. Infidelity is an outlier to this pattern: it typically causes a relational rupture and, if left untreated and unresolved, can erode a couple's relational efficacy and/or lead to the couple's dissolution.

- Fifty percent of people who were unfaithful remain in their marriage. This is truer for men than for women. Partners have many **reasons for opting to stay in the relationship post-infidelity**, including wanting to be with one another, financial considerations, wanting to stay with their children full time, or upholding religious and/or spiritual beliefs and values. Couples generally need to deal with a variety of issues to heal a relational rupture and stay together post-infidelity.

- Infidelity leaves a wake of **emotional distress and trauma** in its path. Depression, anxiety, extreme anger, feelings of betrayal, insecurity, rage, shame, guilt, jealousy, rejection, resentment, fear, and sadness are all common manifestations.

- The hurt partner likely no longer trusts their partner or their relationship post-infidelity, whereas the involved partner may feel shame, guilt, and regret. For the repair process to unfold, **the involved partner must move out of shame and into guilt** so they can focus on their partner and attend to their needs.

- To **reestablish trust**, the involved partner needs to end the infidelity, provide the hurt partner with a full disclosure, demonstrate remorse, atone for their actions, and provide assurances that they won't engage in infidelity again. The hurt partner, in turn, needs to communicate with "I" statements, avoid rehashing the infidelity's details after a certain point, and work towards finding acceptance and offering forgiveness.

- The hurt partner and the involved partner may have **differing perspectives** as to what constitutes infidelity. Finding agreement on this is important for the repair process to be effective.

"Not everything that is faced can be changed, but nothing can be changed until it is faced."

—James Baldwin

"Those who do not turn to face their pain are prone to impose it."

—Terry Real

Chapter 4

Relational Life Therapy

Once both partners understand why infidelity occurred, once the hurt partner offers their partner forgiveness for their transgressions, and once both partners commit to engaging with each other in a more relational manner, they can rebuild their relationship with trust as its cornerstone. From there, they can continue to deepen their relationship and transform it into something better. As Terry Real describes it, once a couple has dealt with the infidelity and done the recovery work, they can settle into a new relationship pattern based on, and entrenched in, the ongoing relational flow of harmony, disharmony, and repair.

A couple that seeks therapy post-infidelity is seeking support as they move through their recovery process. You can help them by 1) providing them with a roadmap to the recovery process, 2) helping them understand what went wrong and what changes are needed to prevent the same thing from happening again, 3) providing psychoeducation that equips them with skills for better communication and more positive interactions, and 4) providing support in pacing themselves as they progress through their recovery process. Using Relational Life Therapy (RLT) as a therapeutic model can make this process easier for you and your clients.

Before you can understand how you can use RLT to do this, you need to understand what RLT is. This chapter provides you with an overview of RLT as a therapeutic approach.

What Is Relational Life Therapy?

Relational Life Therapy (RLT) is a couples therapy approach that Terry Real developed in the 1980s. RLT focuses on improving an individual's relationality — relationality with themself, their partner, and their environment.

RLT's process is divided into three phases, all designed to 1) address a person's individual obstacles (e.g., familial history, personal history, trauma, interpersonal patterns, and lack of skills), and 2) provide remediation so they can live and interact in alignment with full respect living. RLT defines full respect living as pledging that, regardless of what you encounter or what you are experiencing, you'll never fall below the line of respectful behavior to another human being. Refraining from infidelity clearly falls into this category of behavior.

What Is RLT's Theory of Change?

According to RLT, our characters are simply an internalization of our past personal relationships and, more specifically, what we've internalized based on our family experiences and childhood relationships. What was done to us as children, what we observed those we love doing, and what our loved ones allowed us to do to others inform the dysfunctional behaviors and patterns we develop and bring to our relationships as adults. Because RLT believes that our characters (or personalities) are simply the sum of our relationships, it promotes the idea that characterological change is not only possible but can also be swiftly enacted. The following story illustrates how this can play out.

As a young child, Amir frequently watched his parents fight. His father, Caleb, typically yelled at his mother, Imani, whenever he wasn't given what he felt entitled to (e.g., attention, acknowledgment that he was in the right, the food he wanted for dinner). In response, Imani would try and placate Caleb. She'd either give in to whatever Caleb demanded or provide him with whatever need she anticipated he might have. Amir quickly intuited that 1) aggressively demanding that his needs get met, no matter what, has a good chance of getting him what he wants, 2) when this doesn't work, abusing the other person is a good backup, and 3) another person's needs and wants are less important than his own.

By the time Amir was a teenager, he'd mastered his father's relational strategy and applied it when interacting with his mother and sisters. Neither Imani nor Caleb corrected his behavior or even intimated that it was problematic. Later, Amir used these same boundaryless relational tactics with his high school sweetheart and college girlfriends, each of whom left him after confronting him about his behavior and being met with a refusal to change it.

Amir was never too bothered by these relationships' endings, telling himself that each of these women wasn't that important to him since they clearly weren't "the one." Then, he met Laila.

From the beginning, Amir was sure that Laila was the one he wanted to spend the rest of his life with. For the first time, Amir was worried about losing his romantic partner. As a result, he was willing to listen when Laila told him that how he was treating her was unacceptable and that she would leave him unless he changed. Because he was invested in the relationship, Amir not only accepted Laila's feedback, but he also looked for help from an RLT therapist.

Once Amir was motivated and had effective support, he proved to be a quick learner. It wasn't long before he was relating to Laila in a more respectful and relational manner and respecting boundaries. Amir and Laila soon married and happily looked forward to having a child who would not grow up with parents whose interactions were characterized by boundaryless anger and fear.

What Is RLT's Approach?

RLT uses a three-phased approach to effect change. Phase one involves waking up the client, phase two involves family of origin and trauma work, and phase three involves providing psychoeducation. These will be examined in more depth in the next chapter as they relate to infidelity.

Phase One: Waking Up the Client

The first therapeutic phase, waking up the client, involves the therapist confronting their client with the truth about their bad behavior and doing so in such a way that the client feels seen, supported, and understood. It also involves collecting data about the client and their relationship and finding leverage (i.e., something that's meaningful enough to the client[s] to motivate them to commit to the process of change).

Waking up the client allows the therapist to connect with their client(s) in such a way that it becomes easier to help them achieve characterological change. This important component of the first therapeutic phase helps the client own up to their behavior, buy into the idea that they need to change it, and commit to engaging in the change process, all while knowing that it won't be an easy one. When dealing with infidelity, waking up the involved partner is especially important, as it accelerates the couple's post-infidelity repair process.

Phase Two: Family of Origin and Trauma Work

RLT's second therapeutic phase involves doing individual family of origin and trauma work. This work is done in the presence of a person's partner with an eye to releasing trauma from the person and from the person's family system. In this phase, the goal is for the person to face their relational issues and do the healing work required to avoid repeating the same patterns in their current relationship or having them replicated in future generations.

In terms of infidelity, this work is especially important when children are involved. As Dana Weiser has demonstrated, children who grow up in families in which infidelity occurs are likely negatively impacted by it, likely suffer from relational trauma, and are more prone to engaging in infidelity themselves as adults.

As Terry Real likes to say, "Family pathology rolls from generation to generation like a fire in the woods taking down everything in its path until one person, in one generation, has the courage to turn and face the flames. That person brings peace to his ancestors and spares the children that follow." Healing a person's relational traumas not only helps create characterological change, but it also acts as a guardrail against infidelity being transmitted to the person's children and subsequent generations. In essence, it stops the intergenerational transmission of relationally maladaptive patterns. Effectively completing this phase of the work changes the couple's future course and that of others who are impacted by them, including subsequent generations.

Phase Three: Psychoeducation and Skills Development

After trauma is released, the RLT therapist works with the couple on the third and final therapeutic phase: psychoeducation and skills development. This involves teaching each person, and the couple, relational skills (e.g., empathy, accountability, and vulnerability) that allow them to interact in more relational ways and enable their relationship to thrive. In post-infidelity repair, a couple needs to develop these skills to not only survive but to also transform their relationship into a more nourishing and relational one. The goal is to create an environment in which infidelity is no longer an appealing option.

Theoretical Underpinnings

RLT draws on gender studies, systems theory, trauma and recovery work, and neurobiology. Understanding each of these aspects help you, as a therapist, understand how RLT addresses infidelity.

Gender Studies

RLT recognizes political and psychological patriarchy. It assumes that political patriarchy (the systemic oppression of women) is interwoven with and influences our relationships. Specifically, RLT believes that our current patriarchal culture doesn't support relationships. This, in turn, helps explain why most families and romantic relationships are relationally dysfunctional.

Psychological patriarchy is the belief that humans can be divided into two halves based on masculine and feminine qualities and that feminine qualities are valued less than masculine qualities. RLT believes that psychological patriarchy not only exists but also informs much of the dysfunction that exists in relationships. RLT also believes that this is further supported by what it calls the core collusion: whoever is on the feminine side colludes to protect those on the masculine side, regardless of how much they are being hurt by them.

RLT believes that true intimacy and relational living requires breaking the chains of psychological patriarchy and moving beyond traditional gender roles. As a result, as Terry Real likes to say, an RLT therapist's job is to encourage "the mighty to melt and the weak to stand up."

Changing gender-based power dynamics is especially important when dealing with infidelity. In therapy, this involves helping the couple 1) understand the relational power differences (inside and outside their relationship) that may have encouraged the conditions in which the infidelity occurred, and 2) change existing power imbalances within their relationship to create a more equal one.

Systems Theory

RLT is firmly rooted in ecological systems theory. It sees each relationship as a unique system living in its own ecology whose parts are exquisitely interdependent. Each part, or person, has influence on and is influenced by the relationship, their family or origin, and the social and generational systems they come from.

The Relationship

When counseling couples, RLT views the relationship as a system that must be treated in its own right. Just as each individual in the relationship is its own system, so too is the relationship itself a system.

Stance-stance-dance is a tool RLT therapists use to diagnose the relationship on an ongoing basis. It involves identifying each person's relational stance (e.g., righteous offending pursuer, martyred angry victim) and then identifying the relationship's dance (e.g., the more she pursues aggressively, the more he withdraws angrily; the more righteously she pursues him in a disregarding boundaryless manner, the more he withdraws and feels like a victim). Dances are always a combination of pursuit-withdraw, pursuit-pursuit, or withdraw-withdraw. Once identified, the dance itself becomes one of the patients that the therapist treats.

In terms of infidelity, the therapist must identify what each person's stance brings, or fails to bring, to the relationship. How it contributed to creating a system in which infidelity was an option or a desired solution is a key question. Helping clients shift a negative relational stance (e.g., critical and angry pursuing) into a more positive one (e.g., curious and open engagement) can help them create a dance that's more relationally entrenched and doesn't easily lend itself to infidelity.

Family

According to RLT, we all develop our losing relational strategies (i.e., withdrawal, needing to be right, control, retaliation, and unbridled self-expression) in our families of origin. These, along with how we, as children, experienced our parents (grandiose, shame-based, walled off, or boundaryless), inform how we approach our relationships and the relational strategies we use as adults.

Specifically, RLT defines feeling secure and equal to our partner and relating to them as such as being in the circle of health. Feeling insecure and unequal to our partner leads us to feel better than (one up from) or less than (one down from) our partner. When outside the circle of health, we act in ways that are boundaryless or walled off while being anchored in grandiosity or shame. Often, this is when our relationships fall apart. It's for this reason that moving the involved partner from a state of shame to guilt is so important — without this, the involved partner will never be able to approach the hurt partner as an equal, and true repair will never take place.

Social and Generational Systems

Each relationship is itself a unique ecological system, as well as a part of the larger systems in which it operates (e.g., social structures, families, cultures). RLT believes that this larger interdependence is one reason that relational patterns and ways of interacting are transmitted from generation to generation. If we fail to address dysfunctional system patterns, they inevitably replicate themselves. Looking at the whole system and healing generational patterns allows change to occur within the couple and within each person. This is especially important when therapy deals with couples in which infidelity is an intergenerational phenomenon.

Finally, because RLT is grounded in family therapy, it looks not only at the impacts that family members have on one another and on the couple's relationship itself, but also at possible impacts on the children involved. RLT's main goals, aside from improving relationality within the couple, are to heal relational trauma, to stop negative relational patterns from impacting children in the here and now, and to prevent them from being passed along to the next generation.

When treating couples navigating a post-infidelity reality, one of RLT's therapeutic goals is to interrupt the intergenerational transmission of infidelity as an acceptable relational coping strategy. Another is to transform the system (the couple's relationship and the family system as a whole) so that it uses more relational patterns of interaction, ones that encourage all members to stay within the system without involving thirds.

Trauma and Recovery Work

Terry Real often cites Pia Mellody, an addictions counselor at The Meadows, as his mentor and someone who heavily influenced his thinking and RLT's theoretical evolution. As such, RLT is grounded in addictions work.

RLT believes that we are each composed of three parts: a wounded child, an adaptive child, and a wise adult. Both our wounded child and our adaptive child are forged in trauma. The wounded child develops as a result of trauma experienced at a very young age (less than 5 years old) and just wants to be held and reassured. The adaptive child develops later, either due to behavior that was modeled for us or as a reaction against what we experienced when very young.

The adaptive child is a child's version of an adult. It's cobbled together by a child as a survival strategy (e.g., "If I work hard, I'll never have to worry about money"; "As long as I'm physically desirable, I'll know I'm worthy"; "As long as I'm having sex with someone, they'll need me, and I won't be left alone."). The adaptive child is defined by black-and-white thinking, by being perfectionistic, relentless, rigid, harsh, hard, and certain, and by feeling tight in the body.

According to RLT, as adults, we often run our lives through our adaptive child, and society often rewards our adaptive child behaviors (e.g., being a workaholic, overexercising). However, when in charge, the adaptive child typically makes a mess of our relationships (e.g., those who work compulsively often make a lot of money and can afford many symbols of success but frequently have little time for their partners and children). This interpretation implies that people engaging in infidelity might be influenced by or are acting out of their adaptive child.

According to RLT, only when we're in our wise adult can we act relationally and achieve intimacy and connection. The wise adult uses our brain's prefrontal lobes and is defined by nuanced thinking, by being realistic, forgiving, flexible, warm, yielding, and humble, and by feeling relaxed in our body. When we're in our wise adult, we can be curious, be open to unexpected possibilities, are able to speak from our heart, and can accept the reality of our current situation.

RLT focuses on resolving relational trauma, both through inner child work and by unblending someone from their adaptive child and their family of origin so that they can reside in their wise adult. When a person's wise adult is in the driver's seat, they can access and apply newly learned relational skills on an ongoing basis. RLT states that moving into our wise adult and being relational is a process of recovery, one we must consistently engage in over time if we want to live relationally.

Neurobiology

RLT is grounded in neurobiology. A critical skill RLT therapists teach their clients is how to recognize when they're in second consciousness.

RLT defines first consciousness as the knee-jerk reaction(s) we experience when we're being led by our adaptive child. When we're in first consciousness, we're operating out of our amygdala, a part of the limbic system or sub-cortical area. In this moment, we are typically already in a fight, flight, freeze, or fawn response.

When responding from first consciousness, we usually use a less relational approach. We adopt characteristics of black-and-white thinking, perfectionism, harshness, rigidity, relentlessness, and certainty, and, often, feel tightness in our body. These characteristics don't promote relationality. They do, however, characterize how many hurt partners spontaneously respond to an act of infidelity and/or conditions to which involved partners respond with infidelity.

In RLT, the therapist's job is to help clients access their wise adult and display more relational characteristics, such as nuanced, realistic, and subtle thinking, warmth, flexibility, forgiveness, and humility, while allowing their body to remain relaxed. This is called second consciousness. The therapist teaches their clients how to access this part of themselves on an ongoing basis, even when they're flooded or hyperaroused.

A powerful RLT tool involves the therapist staying in their wise adult throughout the therapy session. By doing so, they lend their prefrontal cortex to their clients. This temporarily allows the couple's relationship, an unstable dyad, to become part of a more stable triad system. RLT suggests this encourages quicker resolution of dysfunctional behaviors and increases the couple's levels of relationality.

When healing from infidelity, both the involved partner and the hurt partner must learn to operate from their wise adult and recognize when their adaptive child has stepped front and center. These skills provide a measure of protection against future infidelity by either partner and allow for more meaningful and sincere repair to occur. Therapists can both supply their prefrontal cortex in service of this and use it to model appropriate and positive relational behaviors.

RLT Beliefs About the Therapist's Role

RLT is different from traditional therapy in many ways. Specifically, the RLT approach differs from most other therapeutic approaches in six key areas.

Therapists Confront Their Clients Early On

RLT therapists are encouraged to confront their clients with the truth about their bad behavior early on in the therapeutic process, as they're forming the therapeutic alliance. Rather than viewing confrontation as a risky exercise that may or may not be effective once they've established a solid therapeutic alliance, the therapist uses it as a way of connecting with and entering into a relationship with their client.

A properly conducted confrontation allows a client to feel seen and understood, something that then forms the bedrock of the therapeutic alliance. Having a rock-solid therapeutic alliance from the outset allows the RLT therapist to help the couple move more quickly through their hurt and into relational repair. This is especially true when navigating post-infidelity repair. Here is an example of how this might sound.

 "Stacey, I can see how unhappy you've been in your relationship with Jason. I see how neglected you've felt and how lonely you've been. I know this has gone on for a very long time, making you desperate for connection. You saw your mom engage in infidelity, so looking elsewhere to get your needs met made sense to you.

"I also know you're a really good person who cares deeply about Jason and your kids, and that you don't want to inflict on them the same pain you experienced when your parents divorced after your mom's affair was discovered. You also don't want your kids to repeat this pattern and experience the same pain you're going through now.

"This is a chance for you to do something different and change your familial pattern. Will you let me help you get out of this destructive cycle?"

Therapists Take Sides

In RLT, therapists are encouraged to take sides. Instead of remaining impartial, the therapist sides with the latent (the person with the least amount of power in the relationship) against the blatant (the person who is more relationally dysfunctional and most frequently engages in boundary-violating behaviors, including infidelity). Typically, in cases of infidelity, the hurt partner is the latent.

Who the therapist sides with, however, may change as the couple's relationship dynamic changes and roles reverse. As the involved partner begins to take responsibility and atone, the RLT therapist may take the involved partner's side if the hurt partner isn't receiving the atonement or continues to abuse the involved partner in retaliation for their actions. No matter whose side the therapist is on, the goal is to empower the latent in service of 1) reducing or eliminating negative power dynamics, and 2) improving the relationship by creating greater intimacy, respect, and connection. This goal never wavers even though who the latent is may change at any given time.

Let's go back to Evie and Matt from the last chapter.

Once Matt moved out of shame and into guilt and began exhibiting more relational behaviors, Evie moved out of the latent position and began exhibiting boundaryless behaviors, endlessly castigating Matt for his failings while making unreasonable, impossible-to-meet demands (e.g., that he avoid entering the neighborhood where the woman with whom he'd had an affair lived, even though the neighborhood was the exact territory where he operated his insurance business). Evie was only able to adjust her behavior after the therapist took Matt's side by pointing out how unrealistic these demands were and that continuing to make them was not only negatively impacting the repair process but ultimately blocking her from getting the outcome she so desired.

Quick Characterological Change Is Expected

RLT believes that because our characters are only the sum of our internalized relationships, changes in our relationships allow our character to change. Consequently, characterological change isn't only possible but can be expected and quickly enacted as a couple's relationship changes. This belief is particularly important when dealing with infidelity since it allows the therapist to adopt a stance that the involved person's actions vis-à-vis infidelity aren't their defined character and that both the person, and the couple's relationship, can change.

However, RLT does not state that characterological change alone is enough to ensure that relational change will occur. For relational change to take place, RLT believes that psychoeducation about relational skills is also required. Psychoeducation and skills development is especially important when dealing with infidelity's aftermath since a couple can only rectify many of the relational deficits that may have contributed to the infidelity in the first place by practicing and deploying new skills.

The Therapist's Job Is Not to Nurture Clients

In RLT, the therapist's job isn't to heal their client by nurturing them. Instead, the RLT therapist's job is to heal their clients by equipping them to live relationally. This involves teaching clients how to have relational character traits, such as empathy, accountability, and vulnerability — all qualities that act as antidotes to the temptation of engaging in infidelity.

The therapist accomplishes this by modeling these traits — by being relational with their clients and by adopting the role of coach and fellow traveler — not by being an impartial expert. This requires that the therapist be authentic (dare to speak their truth), be transparent (not hide behind professional neutrality), practice what they preach in all interactions, share their journey (self-disclose while maintaining boundaries), and be explicitly educational without being attached to outcome. Here is an example of how this might sound.

"Jamal, you've been invested in developing more relational behaviors, and Malika was responding. You were practicing the skills you've learned and getting results — Malika was giving you more of what you wanted and needed in this relationship, the very lack of which contributed to you seeking it outside your marriage.

"I've noticed, though, that something's changed in the last few weeks. You're backsliding into your old patterns. You're not communicating your needs, you're treating Malika as if she's the worst version of herself that you can imagine, and you're flying off the handle when you get angry. It seems like the skills we've worked on developing have flown out the window. I don't know if you've lost the motivation to do this work or if something else is going on. But I do know that if you continue on this path, this relationship might continue, but it'll be toxic for both of you. Or it might just implode.

"You might think I'm judging you, but I know what I'm saying to be true from personal experience. Before we learned these same relational skills ten years ago, my husband and I were just like you and Malika. Even today, when we forget to use these skills, we look just as bad as you do. So, Jamal, what do you want to do? I'm rooting for you, and I'll support you, but at the end of the day, it's your marriage and your decision — I get to go home to my happy home and happy life."

Shame and Grandiosity Are Addressed

RLT therapists tackle the issues of shame and grandiosity (with an emphasis on grandiosity) in each person and in the relationship. When someone is suffering from grandiosity, they feel superior to their partner. Correspondingly, when they suffer from shame, they feel they're worth less than their partner. In either state, the person can act in a boundaryless manner or be withdrawn. Both states prevent connection and effective communication. RLT therapy aims to help both partners feel equal to the other for longer periods of time since it's only when equality exists that true connection can occur.

Dealing with shame and grandiosity is especially important in infidelity since the involved partner often feels a sense of entitlement (stemming from grandiosity) about their behavior while engaging in infidelity and shame about it afterwards. Neither of these states are conducive to relational repair.

Individual Trauma Work Is Done Within the Couple

In RLT, each person's trauma work is done in the presence of their partner. This may involve inner child work and/or delving deeply into the inner machinations of their family of origin and childhood relational traumas.

When treating a couple for infidelity, this work helps the involved partner resolve issues that may have contributed to the infidelity. It also helps the hurt partner understand the roots of their partner's behavior while fostering empathy and compassion. Building understanding, compassion, and connection in both the involved partner and the hurt partner creates emotional connection. Consider the following example.

It was only after Micah explored her early childhood in couples therapy that she and her husband, Jackson, were able to understand some of the factors influencing her decision to be unfaithful. Growing up, Micah had not only witnessed her father's infidelities to her mother, but she had also been her mother's sole confidant, privy to all her hurt and pain. Early on, at the age of eight, she'd made a vow to herself that she would never find herself in the same weak and vulnerable position as her mother — loving someone with whom she was desperate to connect, but who kept her dependent and emotionally at bay.

When space developed between her and Jackson, Micah felt more and more lonely and disconnected. She decided she wouldn't wait for Jackson to realize her fears. Instead, she'd take the initiative and have an affair. Beating him to the punch gave her a sense of control and a measure of reassurance that she wouldn't wind up like her mother, crying with raccoon eyes over her empty vodka glass into the late hours of the night.

For his part, Jackson, while exploring his family of origin, realized that although his parents had never been unfaithful to one another, they also weren't emotionally close and that interpersonal conflicts in the home were never directly addressed. Instead, they were swept under the rug.

His mother, with whom Jackson had been close, had focused on the home and raising the children, whereas his father had worked in an executive position, providing amply for the family but rarely interacting with his wife or children. By frequently pointing out that his father was a good provider, his mother had encouraged Jackson to believe that, for a man, being a good partner means bringing home the dough but doing little else.

Having no model for being emotionally connected and for navigating conflict, Jackson found himself pulling away from Micah whenever she wanted to get close or appeared upset. Following this, his response was to double down on trying to earn more money in order to placate her — the very behavior that prompted her to look outside the relationship for connection and emotional satisfaction.

As both Micah and Jackson began to understand the factors that had influenced their behaviors and responses, they also developed greater empathy for each other. This empathy helped bring them out of shame and grandiosity, helped equalize their roles in their relationship, and provided them with the motivation to change their own behaviors as well as support each other while they expanded their skill sets on a somewhat bumpy road.

Summary

Relational Life Therapy (RLT) is a systems approach to couples counseling that not only looks to improve a couple's relationship, but also to transform it into something more relational, democratic, connected, and inspiring for the couple and others impacted by their relationship. An RLT therapist's role is an active one, characterized by authenticity, transparency, and directiveness. All this while straddling the line of holding out hope to the couple that they are capable of so much more while being completely detached from the outcome. This approach is even more rigorous when applied to infidelity. We'll explore this in depth in the next chapter.

TL;DR

- RLT is focused on improving an individual's **relationality** with themself, their partner, and their environment.

- According to RLT, our characters are nothing more than an internalization of our historical personal relationships and, more specifically, what we have internalized as a result of our childhood experiences and our family of origin. Because RLT is predicated on the belief that our characters (or personalities) are simply the sum of our relationships, **characterological change** is not only possible but can also be swiftly enacted.

- RLT has **three therapeutic phases**: 1) waking up the client by confronting them about the truth of their bad behavior, 2) inner child and trauma work done in the presence of the partner, and 3) psychoeducation and skills development.

- RLT recognizes **political and psychological patriarchy** and advocates that true intimacy, and relational living, requires breaking the chains of psychological patriarchy and moving beyond traditional gender roles. RLT looks to eradicate power imbalances within relationships.

- RLT uses a **systems focus**. It looks at the relationship as a unique ecological system needing to be healed. It considers that each person in the relationship is impacted by their own family of origin, which, in turn, was impacted by the family systems in which the parents grew up. Finally, RLT acknowledges that each relationship is not an island unto itself — it's impacted by and has an impact on the larger systems in which it operates, the children currently living within it, and the generations to come.

- Each person is impacted by their **wounded and adaptive child**. The adaptive child is a child's version of an adult, cobbled together as a childhood survival strategy. It's defined by black-and-white thinking, by being perfectionistic, relentless, rigid, harsh, hard, and certain, and by feeling tight in the body. When in charge, the adaptive child often makes a mess of relationships.

- The therapist's goal is to teach each person in the relationship how to reside in their **wise adult** (defined by nuanced thinking, by being realistic, forgiving, flexible, warm, yielding, and humble, and by feeling relaxed in the body) and for each person to apply their newly learned relational skills inside their relationship on an ongoing basis.

- RLT is grounded in **neurobiology**. The RLT therapist teaches clients how to recognize when they are in first consciousness (hyperaroused and reactive) and how to bring themselves to a state of second consciousness (equanimity), where they can self-regulate and interact in a relational manner.

- RLT therapists confront their clients early on so that each client feels seen and understood. This **confrontation** helps establish the therapeutic alliance.

- RLT **therapists side with the latent** (the person with the least amount of power in the relationship) against the blatant (the person who's more relationally dysfunctional and often engages in boundary-violating behaviors, such as infidelity) in service of creating equality within the relationship. As the couple's relationship dynamic changes, roles may reverse. The RLT therapist, however, always sides with the latent in service of the relationship.

- The RLT therapist does not heal clients by nurturing them but rather by teaching them to **live relationally**. RLT therapists accomplish this by modeling empathy, accountability, and vulnerability, by being relational with their clients, and by adopting the role of coach and fellow traveler rather than impartial expert.

- Issues of **shame** and **grandiosity** are addressed.

"Sometimes, we have to be broken down so that we can be built up into what we're actually meant to be."

—YourTango

Chapter 5

Moving Beyond Repair and Into Transformation

"Sometimes, I'd find myself trusting Emelia again, just like I used to," *Bob recalls. "For minutes, and sometimes hours, it felt like the good old days. We'd be laughing, enjoying each other, and when our eyes met, I'd find myself feeling like the luckiest man on earth. I couldn't believe that we were together. And then, I'd be hit with the memory of her infidelity, and I'd be thrown back into reality.*

"I'd remember that I couldn't trust her and part of me would feel like our entire relationship was a charade. I'd feel despairing, wondering if I'd ever be able to get over what she did and ever be able to fully trust her again. In those moments, I couldn't help but wonder 'What's the point?'"

Recovering from infidelity isn't an easy or a linear process. Typically, couples experience a bumpy journey, moving between closeness and distance, trust and distrust, old patterns and new ones. According to RLT, the recovery process is lengthy, typically taking two to five years for the hurt partner to get over the infidelity and for the couple to emerge transformed.

This recovery process is impossible, however, if the involved partner is still engaged in infidelity. RLT recommends that, as the therapist, you make sure that the infidelity is over, or that the involved partner is actively winding it down, before starting to work with the couple. According to RLT, without this certainty, there is a risk that the couple will remain in a state of stable ambiguity (i.e., both partners uncomfortable with the relationship and its uncertainty, but neither ready to be on their own). In this situation, you can't identify leverage for change, and real change won't take place.

RLT believes that contracting with the couple at the outset around the right to maintain confidences and agreeing that the circle of confidentiality surrounds whoever is in the room allows you to assure each person that they can speak their truth without repercussions. This helps create a climate of openness when discussing with the involved partner whether they have already ended the affair or are in the process of actively ending it. Once you establish that the infidelity is over (or is actively ending) and that both partners are committed to doing recovery work, the first of three post-infidelity RLT reparative therapeutic phases can begin.

To effectively engage in this process, however, you must be clear on their own views and biases regarding infidelity so as to prevent issues of countertransference. This is especially important when using RLT since an RLT therapist doesn't just act as empathetic listener, they also act as an active coach and advice-giver throughout the recovery process. This chapter focuses on exploring how you can apply the RLT methodology and techniques to couples who are moving through post-infidelity recovery.

Phase One: The Acute Phase

The Hurt Partner

"When I first found out about Emelia's infidelity, I couldn't focus on anything else," Bob recounts. "I found it hard to sleep, hard to eat, hard to dress myself in the morning, and hard to get off to work. I was devastated. Everything I'd worked for over the past decade no longer made sense. I couldn't trust Emelia. I couldn't trust that the future I thought we were working towards was even in the cards. I couldn't even trust that what I thought was true about us, or her, was true or that

what I thought to be true was reality. For me, everything was called into question. It was awful!"

In this first phase, the RLT therapist's role involves focusing on helping the hurt partner process the trauma they've suffered. Regarding infidelity, RLT defines trauma as the destruction of the hurt partner's basic assumptions about their partner and their relationship.

According to RLT, when the hurt partner discovers the infidelity, their reality is destroyed. Their identity, in terms of who they thought they were and the intimacy they could count on, is shattered. Because the assumption of connection and being part of something bigger is over, they're left feeling as if they are alone and adrift.

Before the couple's recovery work can begin, the hurt partner must recover from this trauma and find a new solid foothold from which they, individually and within their relationship, can move forward. As the therapist, your focus vis-à-vis the hurt partner is to help them 1) be heard, and 2) process their trauma.

Containment

Initially, RLT advises that you act as a container for the hurt partner's grief about the infidelity. You help them process the infidelity and mourn their old relationship. Similar to supporting someone who's grieving a catastrophe, such as the death of a loved one, you help them experience their feelings and survive. This includes making sure they're eating appropriately, sleeping, and getting access to any medication and supports they may need.

As part of this process, you normalize the hurt partner's thoughts, behaviors, and feelings. RLT believes that using "parts" language in this process (e.g., a part of you wants to murder Emelia, a part of you wants to beg Emelia to stay, a part of you wants to leave Emelia, a part of you loves Emelia and understands what brought her to do what she did) is especially useful since it helps the hurt partner keep in mind that 1) their anger and grief are only part of the picture, and 2) these won't determine their relationship's eventual outcome.

Deceit and Trust

While helping the hurt partner process their grief about the deceit, you also help them rebuild trust. According to Terry Real, whereas discovering the infidelity shatters the hurt partner's reality, deceit around the infidelity creates ongoing questions of "How could you do this to me?" and "How can I trust you not to do so again?"

As you work with the hurt partner to reduce their black-and-white thinking (i.e., victim vs. villain, trustworthy vs. not trustworthy), RLT recommends that you also help them move towards adopting an attitude that, although trust was broken, it's something that can ultimately be repaired. During this period, you treat the deceit like an open wound that is the backdrop upon which therapy and healing must take place.

Disclosure

"At first, Bob would follow me around the house, demanding to know all the details about my affair. I couldn't even go to the bathroom without him hounding me. Even though I knew I should answer some, if not all, of his questions, I felt like I was being persecuted. That started to make me angry. Very angry. Angry enough to want to retaliate and make him feel worse — either by not answering or by giving him what he was demanding in a hurtful way." Emelia recounts. *"It was only once we went to therapy and our therapist helped us establish limits around how much I could disclose and how much he could ask in a single session and under what conditions, that I felt safe enough to start giving Bob the real goods."*

When the involved partner provides a full disclosure, the hurt partner can more easily navigate their questions and doubts. This, in turn, expedites the healing process. RLT believes that, as the therapist, you can play an active role in this process by helping to create the conditions in which the involved partner finds it easier to provide a full disclosure. This largely involves working with the hurt partner to establish limits around when (e.g., in the therapist's office, after the kids are in bed) and for how long (e.g., 20 minutes at a time) they can ask questions about the infidelity and reasonably expect the involved partner to participate in answering them.

Placing limits on the hurt partner helps them avoid engaging in grandiose behaviors (e.g., retaliation or unbridled self-expression), behaviors that may or may not have preexisted the infidelity and contributed to it. Essentially, establishing these limits helps prevent reentrenchment of anti-relational behaviors in the relationship's stance, stance, dance.

The Involved Partner

"Initially, when Bob found out I had cheated on him, my first instinct was to lie," Emelia recalls. *"Once it became clear that lying about it, and denying that it had happened, wasn't going to work, I tried downplaying it. Clearly, that didn't work either. The more half-truths I told, the more I got caught in them, and the angrier Bob became. He also felt like he couldn't trust me at all. In retrospect, this makes sense, but at the time, I just felt like a cornered cat.*

"Before I was unfaithful, Bob wasn't willing to listen to me when I'd ask him to change certain behaviors or try and get close to him. Once he found out I had cheated on him and lied, he was even more unwilling to hear what I had to say. I felt like I was in a no-win situation. If I was miserable before my affair, I was even more miserable after it.

"It was only after I decided that this relationship was important to me and that Bob mattered to me, not just as my husband but as a person, that I decided to answer all his questions as humbly and honestly as I could. I was also more willing to be accountable and transparent around my everyday behavior. I started telling him where I was going and with whom to reassure him that I wasn't going to cheat again. This was a game changer for us — he could see I was genuinely sorry and that I was going out of my way to reassure him that he and our relationship are important to me."

As you work with the hurt partner, RLT requires that you also work with the involved partner to establish reassuring behaviors vis-à-vis the hurt partner (e.g., providing a landline number when they travel, sharing access to their emails, texts, and social media accounts). Basically, you work with the hurt partner to reduce behaviors that may have contributed to the infidelity, while working with the involved partner to increase relational behaviors. For example, the hurt partner might need to decrease unbridled self-expression, retaliation, withdrawal, or controlling behaviors, while the involved partner, might need to increase empathy, compassion, curiosity, openness, and warmth.

RLT suggests that your job, as the therapist, is to help foster accountability and empathy for the hurt partner in the involved partner. However, if the involved partner tends to engage in jagged disclosures (i.e., revealing lesser details or admitting to lesser offenses than occurred), it may be difficult to discern whether they are truly regretful about their infidelity and whether it has in fact ended. This type of disclosure can cause the hurt partner to doubt their partner's authenticity and trustworthiness, which, in turn, may stimulate behaviors that make it more difficult for the involved partner to behave in an accountable and empathetic manner.

To curtail this cycle, RLT recommends that you help the involved partner make as full a disclosure as is needed for the hurt partner to stitch up their reality and feel that they're once again walking on solid ground. This requires that you determine the extent of the disclosure that's necessary, as seen through a lens of humanity, all the while keeping an eye on the goal of achieving authenticity on the part of the involved partner.

RLT recognizes that this process is often complex since each partner is likely having very different emotional experiences. Specifically, the involved partner may have contradictory feelings that make achieving authenticity a challenge. They may be feeling any combination of 1) grief at losing their affair partner, especially if it was a long-term affair, 2) relief that the deception is over and that they're no longer living a lie, and/or 3) happiness about being reunited with their partner and family.

Typically, the involved partner also feels remorse and pain for the hurt they've caused their partner and loved ones. RLT cautions that, because of this, they often want to speed through the repair process so they can return to their previous relational status quo. As a result, they may be reluctant to patiently listen to their partner's recriminations and answer questions. Reassuring your couple that they will indeed move through their hurt and pain and come out, together, on the other side in such a way that they will not just survive the infidelity but also be transformed by it helps both partners stick with this process.

The Bigger Picture

"When our families and friends found out about Emelia's affair, most of them took sides. Many of them told me I shouldn't stay with Emelia. I heard people say things like they always knew Emelia wasn't trustworthy and that they were surprised I'd lasted this long. Some told me I should leave her since I could do so much better. The pressure to leave Emelia was intense, and it was hard to remember why I wanted to stay, what I valued in our relationship, and what I loved about Emelia," Bob remembers.

"There were a lot of similarities for me," Emelia chimes in. "Most of my friends knew how miserable I had been before the affair. They'd listened to my complaints about Bob for years and knew how many times I'd tried to talk to him and to get close, only to be rebuffed. They'd also seen how much happier I was when I was having my affair. They said that leaving him was for the best — that I had done all I could do to make my marriage work and that staying only meant going back to the hell I was living in before my affair."

Ultimately, in this phase, RLT advocates that you must act as a container by holding the relationship and each person within it (including friends, family members, and each partner's individual therapist) while setting limits around behaviors and interaction styles. To do this, you and your clients must agree that, regardless of what others (e.g., friends, family members, other therapists) tell them to do, your judgment is the final one. As Terry Real likes to say, you are like a quarterback who leads and determines the plays involved in the relational recovery process.

This agreement is especially important since the hurt partner often needs to talk about their experience of the trauma many times over. In other types of traumas, the injured partner would typically turn to their partner to obtain comfort. In the case of infidelity, however, they can't do so.

RLT also cautions that others, who may be supporting each partner personally, may not support their relationship. In fact, they may place pressure on the hurt partner to leave the relationship (e.g., "I know you've been with her for a long time and that you love her, but you really shouldn't put up with this treatment. You know she's likely to cheat again. And then you'll be devastated all over again. Protect yourself and just leave her now."). Consequently, RLT emphasizes that your job is to ensure that both the hurt partner and the relationship are supported.

Phase Two: The Deep Dive

"As I answered Bob's questions about my infidelity, he saw how sorry I was for upending our lives and for hurting him. He also saw that I was still committed to him, and committed to working through my infidelity so that we could save our relationship. Eventually, a funny thing happened: Bob was able to get curious about me," Emelia says.

"From my perspective, it was his curiosity that got us over the hump and starting to rebuild our relationship. Because his curiosity was tickled, he eventually asked me why I had been unfaithful, and what I had gotten out of it. By being willing to listen to my answers with an open heart and really hear me, not just with his head but with his heart, he started to understand how lonely I had been in our relationship and how much I craved being connected to him.

"Once he saw that this hadn't previously been a possibility — not because I didn't ask for it, but because he kept turning away from me — he was able to take some responsibility for creating the conditions where I felt like the only option I had was to look elsewhere for companionship. Unless I was willing to drown from loneliness. Which I wasn't. Not to be dramatic or anything."

As the hurt partner's grief diminishes and moves from the front burner to the back, the couple shifts into phase two of the healing process. In RLT, having the involved partner admit to the infidelity and say they're sorry isn't enough for healing to occur. Instead, both people must complete an in-depth exploration of the factors that contributed to the infidelity. This entails moving away from a binary idea of victim and villain, which requires mere remorse and forgiveness for healing to occur, and moving towards a more complex and nuanced view that all parties and multiple factors contributed to it.

Both Terry Real and Esther Perel note that failing to acknowledge why a person engaged in infidelity, and what they gained from it (something typically glossed over in other therapeutic approaches), impacts the involved partner's ability to be genuinely remorseful and sincerely apologize — a requirement for the hurt partner's heart to heal. It also fails to create new conditions that safeguard against one of the partners reengaging in infidelity. Ultimately, according to RLT, the goal in this phase is for the involved partner to regain their own and their partner's esteem, and for the hurt partner to heal. It's only once these conditions are established that new relational patterns can emerge.

Exploring Causes of Infidelity

Exploring the causes of infidelity is a delicate task. RLT believes that it requires you to continually frame and reframe the infidelity in such a way that the couple can examine their behavior and/or their relationship in detail to understand why infidelity was the outcome.

Three Reasons for Infidelity

According to RLT, there are three main reasons for infidelity: 1) something is fundamentally lacking in the relationship, or the relationship is a difficult one, 2) there are character deficits in the involved partner (e.g., they are immature, narcissistic, and/or entitled), or 3) the involved partner is responding to a personal existential crisis. Part of your role as the therapist is to help the couple identify root causes and to be upfront in naming them. According to RLT, by stating this truth, you join with both partners and set the stage for change.

Once underlying causes are identified, RLT recommends that you explore the following three components with the couple: 1) normal human weaknesses, 2) the involved partner's character, and 3) the relationship's long-term underlying character. This involves an in-depth look at the relationship's stance-stance-dance and individual issues of grandiosity and childhood trauma (including each partner's adaptive child). Working on these allows both partners to begin to recognize their dysfunctional stances and pivot towards a desire to build more relational skills.

Role of Grandiosity and Shamelessness

"It's funny," Bob muses. "By the time Emelia was ready to be unfaithful to me, she felt like she had no other option. In a way, she saw me as a lost cause and as someone she couldn't approach anymore to discuss her needs. It was as if she saw me as beneath her.

"When I found out about her affair, our roles switched. Knowing how she had failed our marriage vows and how much she had hurt me, she felt deeply ashamed and as if she was worth less than me. I felt the same: I felt completely superior to her. It was only once we were both able to see ourselves and the other as a flawed individual, neither better than nor worse than the other, that we were able to truly start talking as equals who were on the same team."

RLT believes that a person only engages in infidelity if they're in a state of grandiosity or shamelessness since being in either state allows them to have no concern about the consequences of their actions or concern about their actions' impact on others. According to RLT, bringing each partner down from grandiosity (and into a sense of equality) is essential for empathy to emerge. While grandiosity feels good in the moment, it has long-term negative consequences; only by resolving the tendency to slip into grandiosity can either partner meet the other as an equal and take responsibility for their own contribution to the infidelity.

Values

"Yeah," Emelia chimes in. "Once we were on the same team, with both of us wanting our relationship to not only stay intact but to also thrive in a way it hadn't before, we were able to have more in-depth conversations about things that mattered to us, relationship-wise, including the values we hold for ourselves and our relationship."

As part of this exploratory process, RLT recommends that you engage with the involved partner to explore why someone would refuse to cheat (e.g., they want to honor their vows, they don't want to hurt their partner, they don't want to transgress their values or the relationship's values, they don't want to have to look their children in the eyes if their infidelity were to come to light). Identifying what these reasons are for both partners helps them create a new value-based foundation upon which they can rebuild their relationship.

The Bigger Picture

Empowering Reframes

Throughout this process, RLT encourages you to offer empowering reframes. This is especially important for the hurt partner who, viewing the involved partner as essentially immoral, narcissistic, or immature, may react with anger and grandiosity, thereby reversing the blatant and latent roles. In this case, RLT counsels that your role is twofold: 1) help the hurt partner realize that their partner may act in a way that is grandiose, narcissistic, or immature, and that this is inherently changeable, and 2) help stop the hurt partner from acting out of anger and retaliating. You accomplish the latter by reframing retaliation as an act that's damaging to them and, if applicable, to their children.

Grandiosity and Shame

Essentially, RLT advises that your role here is to 1) help both partners stay out of grandiosity and shame and help keep them in the circle of health where they can see one another as equals, and 2) keep both partners in relationship with one another, the only place where repair and love is possible. In this phase, your end goal is to change the nature of the relationship and stop the intergenerational transmission of anti-relational behaviors. As part of this process, RLT notes that you must do transmission-reception work (i.e., develop each partner's ability to receive the new, more relational behaviors that the other is offering) on an ongoing basis.

Expanding Trust

RLT recommends that you, as the therapist, help both partners enlarge the concept of repair to be less precise than simply an apology and forgiveness. You do this by shifting the hurt partner's idea of trust from a black-and-white conceptualization (i.e., I have it or I don't) to the idea that trust exists by degrees and spheres (e.g., I can trust my husband to pay the bills and pick the children up on time, but I can't trust him not to cheat).

One way that trust is rebuilt is for the involved partner to take full accountability for their actions and to be fully transparent. According to RLT, this doesn't mean that they simply offer a full disclosure regarding the infidelity. Rather, the involved partner offers their partner sincere remorse, if not for engaging in the infidelity (since they may not actually regret the infidelity itself), then for the impacts it has had on those they love and care for.

In fact, as Terry Real emphasizes, talking about what the infidelity provided that was lacking in their relationship opens the conversation up to greater honesty and intimacy. This can encourage the relationship to grow and encompass areas previously neglected. Ultimately, in this phase, your job is to hold both partners while they find their voices and assert their wants and needs. As this unfolds, you underline their growth and the distinction between the people and the couple they were and the people and the couple they're becoming.

Phase Three: Transformation

"It was a great turning point," Emelia remembers. "We started spending more time together, getting closer by doing new activities, like kite surfing, that neither of us had ever tried before. We also created little rituals of checking in with each other at the end of the day and making sure to spend at least 30 minutes a day really paying attention to each other. Now, if I feel lonely or neglected and share this with Bob, he doesn't turn away from me.

"I don't think we would have been able to go the distance without learning the new skills our therapist taught us and practicing them every

day. We both come from homes where our parents weren't attuned to each other and conflict was mismanaged. Getting to the point of understanding and forgiveness was important, but developing skills was instrumental to our success. Our recommitment ceremony to each other by the beach with all our friends and family there didn't hurt either!"

"Life has never been better," Bob interjects. "I never thought I'd say this, and it probably sounds crazy, but Emelia's affair was probably the best thing that ever could've happened to us."

The third and final phase is transformation. It involves transforming both partners' characters so that they can create a new relationship based on a higher level of relationality, satisfaction, and intimacy. RLT believes that true intimacy is predicated on commitment, democracy (a union of equals), and the desire to engage fiercely with another in service of the relationship; until love avoidants and co-dependents are transformed, true intimacy isn't possible, and relational satisfaction will remain low.

To achieve transformation, the couple must move beyond hashing out the infidelity's ins and outs and begin to cement new relational skills into their characters and into their relationship. RLT deems psychoeducation to be a huge part of this process.

As issues are addressed, and as the couple understands not just what happened but why it happened, you provide psychoeducation to increase both partners' relational skills (e.g., how to speak up for what they want, how to speak cleanly and with respect, how to stay in relationship, how to say their truth, how to articulate their needs, how to negotiate). This leads to a change in dysfunctional relational stances and to a greater understanding of the value of long-term relational satisfaction over immediate gratification.

The following are some examples of specific types of relational skills that RLT therapists teach.

Time-Outs

The goal of a time-out is to stop a negative situation from escalating. A person calls a time-out from the relationship to give themself a time-out for the benefit of the relationship. It isn't a weapon to be used against the relationship.

When a time-out is called, both partners stop interacting with one another and take a break from each another by physically moving into separate spaces. The person who calls the time-out checks back in with their partner at predetermined intervals (i.e., 20 minutes, one to two hours, half a day, a day, overnight, etc.). The check-in can take place in person, by phone, or by text. If either person needs more time at the moment of check-in, they let their partner know and commit to checking in at the next preestablished interval.

The goal of a time-out isn't to avoid a hot topic. Instead, the goal is for both partners to come back to the topic when cooler heads can prevail and both partners are regulated and operating from their wise adult. At that time, they can navigate the sticky issue from a place of calm, instead of reactivity, while being centered and connected.

The Feedback Wheel

The feedback wheel is a variant of nonviolent communication, a technique initially developed by Marshall Rosenberg. The feedback wheel is used to communicate thoughts and emotions around a sticky subject. It involves four distinct steps, each completed in one or two sentences:

1) State what you saw or heard (as if reporting a recorded scene).

2) State the story you made up about the event.

3) State how you feel when you think about your story.

4) Request what you'd like your partner to do to change the situation.

"I can still remember the first time I used this technique with Emelia. What a difference it made!" Bob recalls. "Instead of hounding her about where she was going and who she was going to be with, I said, 'Honey, when you went out yesterday without telling me where you were going, I made up the story that you might be out with another man or someone who didn't approve of us trying to work things out. I also made up the story that you didn't care enough about me or our marriage to

make sure that I felt at ease. When I had these thoughts, I started to feel scared that our marriage might be on its last legs and upset that I'm not a priority for you. Honey, I really don't want to feel this way. What I want is to feel that I trust you, trust our marriage, and trust that I'm important to you and that you consider me and my feelings. Because I want to feel this way, I'm asking you to just talk to me before you go out and let me know where you're going and who you're going out with. Would you be able to do that for me?' I couldn't believe it when she paused, thought about it, and said yes!"

The Five Winning Strategies

The five strategies for positive relationships are the opposite of the five losing relational strategies (unbridled self-expression, control, needing to be right, retaliation, and withdrawal). The five winning strategies are

1) making requests instead of complaining to your partner;

2) speaking with and from a place of love;

3) responding with generosity;

4) empowering your partner; and

5) cherishing your partner.

Core Negative Image (CNI) Busting Behaviors

A core negative image (CNI) is the image that each partner has of the other when that person is at their worst. Imagine seeing someone through smoky-colored glasses — the opposite of the rose-colored glasses we all wear in our own relationship's honeymoon phase. Through our smoky-colored glasses, we expect to see, and do see, the worst version of our partner.

CNI busting behaviors require that each partner is clear about their CNI of the other person and the behaviors that reinforce it. Once each partner is clear on this, they share their CNI about their partner with them. Together, the partners draw up a list of behaviors that each person can do to counteract the other person's CNI of them. Each person is responsible for decreasing their CNI reinforcing behaviors and increasing their CNI busting behaviors.

The Repair Process

Because successful relationships are characterized by the cycle of harmony, disharmony, and repair, both partners must learn how to engage in repair post-conflict. RLT provides a three-step process for facilitating repair that involves

1) speaking with love and listening with an open heart;

2) responding with a big-hearted spirit; and

3) encouraging and supporting one another throughout the process.

The Bigger Picture

In this final phase, RLT encourages you to act as a coach to help your clients develop skills and establish contracts around how they want their relationship to unfold. As each partner enacts new relational stances (e.g., curiosity and openness instead of harshness and judgment) and the relationship changes form, you shift from guide to champion and cheerleader and you amplify the couple's progress. Ultimately, your role is to empower each person, and the relationship, so that the flagpole around which they dance is fierce intimacy.

Once the partners' characters and their relationship have transformed, RLT recommends that the couple engages in a ritual to demarcate the old from the new. You can help them determine what is meaningful to them. For some, the ritual may involve literally putting the infidelity behind them (e.g., burning mementos related to the infidelity). For others, the ritual may involve creating a threshold between their old relationship and their new one (e.g., new vows or a new wedding). Whatever the ritual chosen, the act represents a concrete commitment to leave the old relationship, patterns, and habits behind and focus on a future geared towards intimacy, respect, equality, and relational living.

Summary

As a therapist, you can make a difference to a couple's relational trajectory. Your presence and participation in the process, however, isn't enough. The process you adopt and the issues you help the couple address and resolve (i.e., betrayal and trust, guilt and shame, anger, resentment, communication breakdowns, differences in perspectives, and emotional distress) all impact whether a couple will separate or, if not, how their relationship will unfold post-infidelity.

The RLT approach addresses individual and relational dysfunctions so that partners' relational stances are adjusted to more healthy ones geared towards generating intimacy and harmony. Using this approach allows you to address critical factors that determine whether partners remain in an acrimonious relationship, remain committed but no better off than before, or emerge transformed from the experience of infidelity.

TL;DR

- It's imperative that the involved partner has ended, or is in the process of ending, their infidelity for the recovery process to be successful. The **recovery process takes two to five years**.

- The **RLT recovery process has three phases**: 1) the acute phase, 2) the deep dive, and 3) transformation.

- The **therapist's role in the acute phase** is to 1) listen to the hurt partner and help them feel heard, 2) help the hurt partner process the trauma they've suffered as a result of the infidelity, 3) act as a container for each person's feelings and for the relationship, 4) help the involved partner provide a full disclosure and establish limits for the hurt partner to ask questions, 5) help the involved partner establish behaviors that reassure the hurt partner, and 6) work with both partners to reduce anti-relational behaviors and increase relational behaviors.

- The **second phase focuses on an in-depth exploration of the factors that contributed to the infidelity** so that both partners can deeply understand why it took place. This moves the partners towards a more complex and nuanced view that multiple factors and all parties contributed to it. The relationship's **stance-stance-dance** and individual issues of **grandiosity** and **childhood trauma** (including each partner's adaptive child) are examined in depth so that both partners begin to recognize their dysfunctional stances and pivot towards using more relational skills.

- The **final phase involves transforming** both partners' characters and their relationship to create a new one based on more relationality, satisfaction, and intimacy. **Psychoeducation** about relational skills is a key component. As the couple becomes more relational in this phase, the therapist's role shifts from coach to cheerleader. Once the relationship is transformed, the couple can conduct a ritual to demarcate the new relationship from the old.

"Perfection does not exist — you can always do better, and you can always grow."

—Les Brown

Chapter 6

The Highs and Lows of Using RLT

RLT isn't the only therapeutic approach advocating that a couple can create positive relational transformation after infidelity. PACT, Esther Perel, and Gottman, among others, all promote the same belief. With hundreds of therapeutic approaches, and more emerging every year, it's hard to analyze the approaches and determine what makes one better than another, especially when treating a specific issue, such as infidelity.

As good as RLT sounds, it's always nice to have a solid footing to stand on when deciding whether to use a specific approach. "Well, it sounds good and makes intuitive sense" just isn't enough. This chapter provides a concrete evaluation of RLT's pluses and minuses, particularly as applied to navigating the issue of infidelity, so that you have a better basis upon which to decide whether and how you want to use RLT.

RLT Strengths

RLT has several strengths in terms of helping couples not only recover from infidelity but also evolve in its aftermath.

Focuses on the Relational System

RLT's focus on the relational system is holistic. This is especially advantageous when helping couples move beyond infidelity. RLT reveals a complex picture by looking at the relationship as a system, at the larger systems in which the relationship operates, and at the systems in which each person was forged. As the couple engages in the post-infidelity repair process, layered issues associated with their unique multifaceted reality are revealed, peeled away, and addressed.

Contains a Clear Roadmap

RLT explains the reparative phases through which the couple, as a system, must travel to reach post-infidelity relational transformation. These phases and signposts provide a clear roadmap the therapist can use to guide the couple through a thorny and often complex recovery.

Specifically, the RLT roadmap provides the therapist with 1) signposts to determine the couple's current phase, 2) a list of issues that must be addressed, 3) therapeutic stances to use within each phase, and 4) specific relational skills that must be mastered to effect a systemic transformation. With these tools, a therapist is well equipped to act as guide, sounding board, and coach throughout this transformative process.

Incorporates Gender Issues and the Patriarchy

RLT addresses hidden power imbalances by addressing gender issues that originate in the wider society and, consciously or unconsciously, permeate the relationship. Addressing and redressing issues arising from patriarchy allows for greater equality between partners to emerge so that a true collaborative relationship can develop. Only this type of relationship can allow both partners' needs to be met, thus limiting the likelihood that infidelity will be seen as a viable alternative to relational dissatisfaction.

Rooted in Neurobiology

Much of RLT's theory, especially its theory of change, can be mapped to established neurobiology. This lends RLT a particular validity and credibility.

Knowing how maladaptive behaviors develop and why people behave in maladaptive ways that work against relational cohesiveness, even when they know better, allows a therapist to provide clients with informed interventions. It also guides the teaching of relational skills that help clients become more relationally adept, even when in an activated state. By providing ongoing coaching to clients about using these skills while establishing feedback and accountability mechanisms, they come to not only understand the skills conceptually but to also develop the associated behaviors.

The consistent development and use of relational skills promotes proactive communication and helps establish healthy relational boundaries. Over time, partners move from using these skills with conscious awareness and purposive intent to profiting from them as habits that are simply a relational trait.

Mastery of these skills enables each partner to have more of their needs and wants met on an ongoing basis. Ultimately, this contributes to relational joy — a primary bulwark against infidelity.

Incorporates Trauma and Recovery Work

Trauma Work

RLT looks at relational trauma to help partners address issues from their past (e.g., abandonment, familial history of infidelity). These traumas may be influencing their present-day anti-relational behavior, which, in turn, may have contributed to their (or their partner's) infidelity. If left unresolved, the person is at risk of again committing, or being subjected to, infidelity.

As well, long-standing and ingrained issues are addressed with both partners present so that each person can develop empathy for, and understanding of, the other as they engage in this deep and vulnerable work. By addressing relational issues and encouraging new ways of being, the couple begins to see an alternative path forward, one that's more relationally entrenched. This gives them hope that they can achieve an outcome that's different from their past experiences. All this contributes to breaking the chain of relational dysfunction that typically runs through generations.

Recovery Work

RLT's recovery model encourages people to see that their efforts at change lie on a continuum rather than on a fixed point. Each person, and the couple, can feel hope and encouragement that they're not expected to achieve and maintain relational perfection. Instead, they can assume that they will each make mistakes, that repair is possible, and that engaging in ongoing relational repair will allow them to have a functional relationship in which fidelity is assumed.

Encourages Rapid Relational Change

RLT encourages a quick shift in behaviors, thus reducing overall time and dollar investment. It also encourages therapists to provide couples with psychoeducation and concrete skills they can apply outside the therapy room. Both help move people from a conceptual understanding of what their problems are towards sustained behavioral changes that eliminate them. This is especially important for the issue of infidelity, where healing and transformation depend on change in each person's interactional patterns and relational expectations.

Promotes Inclusivity

RLT has looked at issues of diversity, equity, inclusion, and belonging since 2022. Recently, as highlighted in an email Terry Real sent out to the RLT community, RLT has expanded the definition of patriarchy to include any type of oppression, including issues affecting BIPOC and LGBTQ communities, in an effort to improve inclusivity.

Ultimately, RLT is not about judging differences, but about improving relationality and the relational ecosystems in which we humans live. It places an emphasis on equality and respect —

something that crosses all divides. Equality and respect are essential for a couple's relationship to not only work effectively but to also transform it into a more relational entity post-infidelity.

RLT Limitations

Although RLT has many strong positives on its side, it's not a perfect approach. Knowing some of RLT's downsides helps you be better prepared to decide whether and how to apply it to couples dealing with infidelity. The following is a quick overview of RLT's limitations vis-à-vis its approach to post-infidelity relational repair.

Lack of Evidence of Effectiveness

RLT has been used since the 1980s and, according to Terry Real, who has articulated this position in many online trainings, can promote quick and lasting change, sometimes in as little as one session. Many of his claims, however, seem to be based on his own clinical experience with a primarily well-educated and well-heeled group of clients who can afford to pay his hourly fee — one that is higher than the average therapist's. Anecdotally, many RLT therapists charge fees in the higher range of recommended fee guides or, like Terry Real, even higher. Clients who can pay these fees don't represent the wider population, and it's unclear whether treatment of this targeted population positively skews Terry Real's stated RLT results.

Terry Real also claims that 1) other RLT therapists experience the same results, and 2) it's hard to refer people to RLT therapists because their high demand (due to these results) has led to many having limited available hours. The former claim, however, is not supported by empirical evidence, and the latter claim may be partially explained by the relatively small number of certified RLT therapists available until now.

Finally, although many RLT therapists have publicly made statements as to RLT's efficacy, there's currently no evidence-based research supporting claims about its effectiveness. While the Relational Life Institute is planning evidence-based research studies, these are still pending. Positive results of this type of study would validate efficacy claims and determine whether RLT is equally efficacious across cultural and socio-economic groups and relational problems (e.g., infidelity, conflict).

Certification and Practitioner Skill Level

Until recently, many existing certified RLT therapists were trained by Terry Real in an ad hoc manner without proper certification criteria (i.e., practicums, supervision, or formalized assessments). Most training was conducted in the United States (Terry Real's own culture) by Terry Real himself without clear measures and standardization.

Now, The Relational Life Institute is responsible for certification and is in the process of revamping RLT training and certification. As of 2025, this process is still under development and being fine-tuned. Understanding how to apply RLT theory to infidelity and showing that the practitioner can apply it to infidelity is not currently required to attain RLT certification. As a result, it's unclear how RLT therapists' successes are being measured, and whether RLT therapists' successes in treating infidelity can be attributed to RLT.

Furthermore, RLT training for infidelity is divided between two separate courses (*Working with Infidelity in Couples Therapy* audio book and *Working with Infidelity* video course). The content of these courses sometimes overlaps, sometimes dovetails, and is sometimes at odds with the other. Until there's consistency in RLT training and certification requirements and agreement on how RLT should be practiced, especially as it relates to infidelity, designing evidence-based research that can provide positive results will be difficult.

Lack of Tools

Tools to Help a Person Remain in Their Wise Adult

One of RLT's key therapeutic activities is doing inner child work with clients. This experiential activity helps a person get to know and relate to their adaptive child. RLT believes that this familiarity helps a person to recognize the difference between when they're acting from their wise adult versus from their adaptive child. According to RLT, nurturing a person's relationship with their adaptive child over the long run helps ensure that their wise adult is in charge more often than not. This is important since RLT advocates teaching people to deal with conflict and triggering issues only when they're residing in their wise adult.

To this end, RLT therapists teach their clients to establish solid boundaries, breathing exercises, taking time-outs when they notice their adaptive child taking over, and using the feedback wheel to communicate their needs in a respectful manner. They encourage the client to use these tools to help maintain a level of respectful living and to avoid triggering their own or their partner's adaptive child.

Although RLT practitioners teach clients how to recognize their adaptive child, RLT offers few practical skills or tools, aside from breathing, to promote self-regulation, and remembering love, to help them remain in their wise adult. Paradoxically, a person can only access their prefrontal cortex and use these tools when in their wise adult. This creates a catch-22 for people engaged in conflictual interactions. Further, when the adaptive child is triggered, a person may see infidelity as a more attractive solution for achieving connection and relational gratification than staying connected with their partner to work through their existing problems.

Tools to Identify Strength of Current Relationality

RLT doesn't provide the therapist or the couple with tools to determine the partners' level of connection/disconnection on an ongoing and moment-by-moment basis. Failing to take this relational pulse on a regular basis creates ample opportunity 1) for partners to become disconnected from one another without awareness, and 2) for a disconnected state to slowly infiltrate the relationship and become the new norm. A prolonged, deep, and unrepaired disconnection creates rich soil for infidelity to recur.

Tools to Establish Common Values and Breathe Relational Life Into Them

Although RLT refers to the importance of relational intimacy and the importance of a common understanding of the relationship's boundaries, it doesn't specify how to develop a clear relational boundary. It also doesn't provide any tools to 1) help a couple determine mutual values-based goals (e.g., regarding what monogamy looks like for both parties), or 2) assess their progress towards achieving these goals.

Tools to Navigate Post-Conflict Repair

RLT doesn't provide couples with tools or skills, beyond the feedback wheel and the five winning strategies, to negotiate conflict based on differing wants and needs and to jointly find a novel solution, all while honoring shared and individual values. Such tools would be particularly helpful for issues of infidelity and intimacy.

Summary

No theoretical therapeutic approach is perfect. In general, therapists decide to use those that resonate the most with them on a personal level. Having an idea of any approach's strengths and limitations lets you make this decision more sagely and apply the approach with greater intention, knowing all the while that you may need to supplement it with tools, techniques, and interventions derived elsewhere.

This is equally true for RLT. As an approach, RLT has many strengths and several limitations. It's an approach that allows you to confidently treat a couple post-infidelity, knowing that partners who successfully move through RLT's three reparative phases have a good chance at transforming their relationship into one that's more relational, connected, intimate, and joyous. Although RLT has limitations, it's also an approach that's flexible enough to accommodate the integration of other tools, techniques, and interventions. We turn to this next.

TL;DR

- Hundreds of theoretical approaches exist, with many new ones emerging each year. Knowing an **approach's strengths and limitations** allows you to apply it more effectively and with intent. This is especially true when dealing with infidelity.

RLT's Strengths

- RLT's system focus allows a **nuanced picture** of a couple's issues to emerge and for issues to be addressed in an in-depth manner.

- RLT provides a therapist with a **clear roadmap** to help guide couples through their repair process. This roadmap contains three clear reparative phases needed for transformation to occur.

- By addressing **gender and power imbalances**, couples can create a more equal and collaborative relationship moving forward. This allows each partner's needs to be met, thus reducing infidelity's appeal as a solution to relational dissatisfaction.

- RLT's **roots in neurobiology** lend it validity and credibility. It allows therapists to provide clients with informed interventions and to teach them relational skills for becoming more relationally adept, even when in a hyperaroused state. Coaching and feedback help each person develop these skills so that they become part of the fabric of who they are.

- RLT's focus on completing **trauma and recovery work in the presence of the person's partner** helps foster empathy and engender hope that a different type of relationship is possible. Treating change as lying on a continuum also sets the stage for a couple to see that a great relationship isn't about perfection, but about the ability to engage in the repair process and move forward together.

- RLT focuses on **rapid behavioral change** so that clients gain concrete relational skills while spending less time and money compared to traditional therapies.

- RLT defines **patriarchy as any type of oppression**, including issues affecting BIPOC and LGBTQ communities. This makes it highly inclusive and allows for power dynamics within various relational ecosystems to be addressed.

RLT's Limitations

- RLT's claims of rapid behavioral change and efficacy are based on Terry Real's own clinical experience, which is largely focused on well-educated people with high net worths. These **claims are not backed by evidence-based research.**

- Certified RLT therapists aren't required to undertake training on infidelity, nor are they evaluated on their understanding of how to treat infidelity. This may lead to considerable variability among practitioners and contribute to **difficulties in assessing efficacy.**

- RLT **provides limited tools** for therapists to teach people how to stay in their wise adult when triggered, how to identify the strength of their current relationality, how to establish common values, and how to navigate post-conflict repair.

"Intimacy is being seen and known as the person you truly are."

—Amy Bloom

"Curiosity is one of the greatest secrets of happiness."

—Bryant H. McGill

Chapter 7

Tools, Tools, and More Tools

Although RLT outlines three clear phases that a couple needs to move through to achieve post-infidelity relational transformation, its approach is malleable. This flexibility allows you to overlay each RLT phase with other tools and interventions.

The Connected Hearts Inspire (CHI) Relationship Map (originally developed by me and Matthew Gould as the HTI Relationship Map for leadership purposes) is a relationship roadmap that contains tools you can both use and teach your clients to use throughout the reparative process to create a more positive outcome. Specifically, using the CHI Relationship Map and its tools allows partners to 1) recognize when they're becoming more distant and disconnected from each other, 2) stay in their wise adults, 3) resolve conflicts more relationally, and 4) move towards one another to achieve co-created relationship goals, including those aimed at creating a relationship based on monogamy, trust, and intimacy.

This chapter explores how you can integrate the CHI Relationship Map and its tools into an RLT approach when counseling couples who are knee deep in the post-infidelity reparative process and longing for relational transformation.

The Connected Hearts Inspire (CHI) Relationship Map

The CHI Relationship Map (below) contains six tools (boundaries, full responsibility, awareness, STCI, the four relationship cornerstones, and the relationship stake), all of which are explored in depth below. You can teach each of these to your clients to help them remain in their wise adult. This makes guiding them through post-infidelity repair easier. When applied, these tools also help partners develop relational skills that increase their relational satisfaction, prevent a reoccurrence of infidelity, and transform their relationship into one that's based on deeper intimacy and respect.

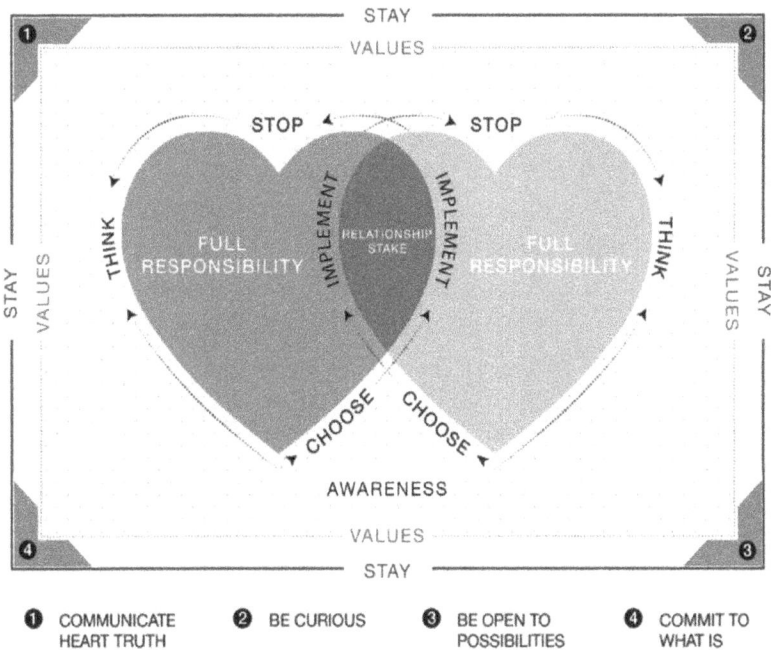

The CHI Relationship Map

Boundaries

Relationships need containing walls. Boundaries provide them. Although boundaries are important for any relationship's success, they're even more important in intimate relationships.

Since each partner may see a different ideal form and shape for their relationship's containing wall, it's important that partners work together to mutually establish the type of relationship they're in and who belongs in it. Once established, this agreement provides all partners with clear guidelines about 1) permissible and expected behaviors within their relationship, and 2) expectations regarding commitment when difficulties arise. The CHI Relationship Map provides partners with clear elements on which to focus when engaging in this process. These are 1) stay, and 2) values.

Stay

Stay refers to the relationship boundary's outer perimeter and a person's commitment to stay in relationship with their partner, stay in relationship with themselves and their emotions, and stay in the situation and the moment, even if they need to elongate the pause between stimulus and response.

Although the commitment to stay refers to staying no matter what shows up, staying is always a choice: A person always has the freedom to adopt or reject it. For example, if violence were to occur, stay does not imply that a person should stay in the situation or relationship. A person's commitment to stay doesn't negate their freedom to choose to leave should it become clear that staying is a harmful choice.

In the diagram above, stay is depicted as a solid line because, to be effective, it can't be crossed; conflict resolution is impossible if one person refuses to stay engaged with their partner. Engagement can mean being physically and/or emotionally connected. For example, as John Gottman has clearly articulated, stonewalling is a clear form of disengaging from the other person and/or relationship. When it becomes part of a relationship's fabric, it almost always indicates that the relationship's demise is near.

However, staying doesn't mean being actively engaged in a heated conflict. Instead, it involves honoring a commitment to stay in relationship with the other person, and/or the issue when facing an uncomfortable situation, even if taking a breather or a pause is needed.

Stay's purpose is to protect a relationship's boundaries so partners can deal with the current conflict or disharmony collaboratively, without threat from a third. Helping partners get clear on this commitment, and what it looks like, helps them reduce the risk of infidelity, especially when their relationship is tense or fueled by disconnection.

Values

Values are the elements we believe are worthwhile and important: They provide meaning to our lives. Values are not absolute and can't be universally applied since their importance and relevance are personal and individual. They tend to reflect a person's belief systems and are sometimes inherited, thus reflecting their history and sense of community. Whether articulated or not, values influence how people behave, how they feel, how they respond to situations, and how they interact with their loved ones.

In the CHI Relationship Map, values create the relationship's inner boundary. They refer to all the values that impact a relationship, including each partner's personal values (e.g., trust, authenticity, social status), as well as the values the relationship takes on as part of its identity (e.g., monogamy, transparency, intimacy). These values may be overtly known by both partners, or covert and implicit, hidden to one or both partners, and even to the individuals themselves.

The CHI Relationship Map uses a dotted line to represent values and to indicate that a relationship's inner boundary wall is permeable. When a person or a relationship's values are transgressed, the relationship may not only survive but thrive if partners engage in appropriate repair. This repair process involves 1) addressing the transgression, 2) identifying the values that were trampled on, 3) identifying the values that need to be honored for each person to move forward in positive relationship, 4) committing to concrete actions that allow this to happen, and 5) recommitting to honoring the identified values.

Boundaries and Infidelity

When recovering from infidelity, you can help partners commit to staying engaged with each other throughout the process. This commitment is different from a commitment to move forward as a couple once the process is complete. Rather, it's a commitment to engage full-heartedly in the repair process and deal with issues that emerge without engaging in grandiose or withdrawing behaviors. This type of commitment falls squarely in line with RLT's idea of full respect living.

Engaging in this commitment gives each partner time to identify their core values and determine if they align with previously identified values, both spoken and unspoken, especially concerning the issue of monogamy and fidelity. They can use this lens to examine their assumptions and expectations about this issue and process the resulting hurts and disappointments that occurred when their values were transgressed.

As partners engage in this exploration, they can work together to establish 1) the values they want to adopt as center points for their relationship, 2) how they will strive to honor them, and 3) how they can identify when their values are being fulfilled or transgressed. These criteria help partners create a strong foundation to ground their relationship in an intimacy derived from agreement on how their relationship will look if successful and insight into what is deeply meaningful to each person.

Solid and agreed-upon boundaries help protect a relationship from thirds that may negatively influence it. They also serve as a reference point that each partner can use to identify where they lie in relation to the other person. Partners can use solid and agreed-upon boundaries as a benchmark to determine whether they are closer and more connected (i.e., farther away from the boundary's edge) or farther apart and more disconnected (i.e., closer to the boundary's edge).

With infidelity, this is particularly useful since a solid and agreed-upon relationship boundary provides each partner with an impartial tool they can use at any time, on their own or together, to determine their risk of violating their relationship's boundaries. Ultimately, it can serve as an early warning signal that can help each partner, and the couple itself, to avoid veering off their desired path. The following illustrates how this works in action.

"You know," Bob muses, "Emelia and I got married when we were really young. We met in our first year of college and then just kept going. By the time we married, we'd been together for a long time, and it just seemed like the logical next step.

"Although we both knew we eventually wanted to have a family, we'd never really discussed what each of us expected from the other person, or the relationship, over the long term. Heck, we didn't even know what was truly important, to ourselves or each other. In retrospect, even though we thought we were grown up, we were really just babies when we got married, still figuring out who we were and our place in the world.

"For me, I just assumed that married life would look like my parents' relationship, with a few tweaks. It never even crossed my mind that a committed relationship could look any other way, and it certainly never crossed my mind that Emelia would go outside our marriage if she was unhappy. I guess I just assumed that if she was unhappy, she'd put her energies into work, the kids, or her friends to compensate, like my mom did, and that we'd eventually figure it out. Her affair was a rude awakening! And it's been a blessing in disguise.

"Since we started therapy, I've gotten to know Emelia better, and myself as well. I've learned that I have core values of monogamy, fun — which, honestly, I didn't even know was important to me until our relationship became markedly unfun — and connection. It was revealing to learn that Emelia has core values of connection, creativity, and authenticity.

"Learning about these made me realize how far she must have strayed from herself in our marriage and how much I contributed to it by taking her for granted, living our life as if on a hum-drum schedule,

and shutting her out. With hindsight, I can now see that by the time Emelia decided to have an affair, she no longer felt like herself and that, although having the affair betrayed our marriage, it stopped Emelia from betraying herself since it gave her the opportunity to lean back into her core values, the values that make her her.

"The other thing I realized as we identified our core values is how much Emelia and I have in common, and how honoring each other's values as part of our relationship actually helps each of us honor our own. For example, when I relax and buy into what Emelia's proposing, even if it sounds crazy, engaging in her creativity makes my life (and our relationship) more fun!"

"From my point of view," Emelia interjects, "Once I realized Bob was willing to engage with me and that I wasn't stuck in a suffocating marriage that had no chance of changing, I was more than willing to honor Bob's value of monogamy. Truthfully, it's one of mine too, provided it doesn't require that I give up on my own core values. Now, I can see the value of staying inside the marriage and working things out so that we can get to a better place, together."

Full Responsibility

The CHI Relationship Map is based on the idea that each partner is always 100% responsible for 1) their own thoughts and actions, and 2) their relationship. This is called full responsibility.

Full responsibility differs from fault. Whereas fault involves blame, full responsibility involves a person owning their choices, and the impacts of their choices, and doing whatever is needed to address any resulting problem or to improve their relationship.

In the CHI Relationship Map, full responsibility lies in four domains. These are responsibility for 1) our self, 2) our impact on our partner, 3) our relationship, and 4) our relationship's impact on the environment around it.

Full Responsibility for Self

Full responsibility for self involves each person taking responsibility for their feelings, thoughts, and actions. It requires that a person recognize when their feelings, thoughts, or actions don't line up with their values, vision, and purpose, and that they make the adjustments required to be congruent. Consider the following example.

Once Emilia realized that monogamy was not only one of her values, but one of Bob's core values, as well as one of their relationship's, she said, "Now, if I find myself attracted to a co-worker who's inviting me to discuss a pressing business problem over dinner, I decline since it might lead to a situation in which I might be tempted to act against my value of monogamy."

Full Responsibility for the Other(s)

Full responsibility for impact on the other person(s) involves each person taking responsibility for the impact they're having on the other person(s) in their relationship. It involves 1) adjusting their actions when their impact, intended or not, is detrimental to their partner, and 2) doing so without blaming their partner or making excuses for their own behavior. Consider the following example.

Emelia recounts how she's now more aware of how her own actions can impact her relationship and willingly makes changes accordingly. "Work's been stressful lately and I've been very irritable, trying to take time for myself wherever I can. Bob's been getting upset when I just disappear without telling him, even if it's just to the other room. The more upset he gets, the more I just want to withdraw. Old habits die hard, I guess.

"Unlike in our earlier years, I was able to see that this pattern was causing us to disconnect from each other, and that the way I was going about trying to get my needs met was hurting him. Realizing this made me want to find another way of getting my needs met, or to continue doing what I was doing in a way that made Bob feel good. He's the one I love after all!"

Full Responsibility for the Relationship

Full responsibility for the relationship involves a person 1) taking responsibility for the impact their actions have on their relationship, and 2) taking steps to repair any damage they've inflicted on it, regardless of what their partner has contributed to the situation. It also consists of a person taking full responsibility for maintaining their relationship's health and integrity, regardless of what their partner does or doesn't do. The following story illustrates how this can play out.

As Emelia recalls, "Bob was devastated by my affair. The guy didn't mean that much to me, but now I can really see why Bob was so upset and why he was talking to me the way he was when he first found out. At first, it felt kind of unreasonable. I mean, I didn't even think he'd care.

"Then, I realized how much I'd messed up and how important our relationship and marriage are to me. I realized I wanted to be in it for the long haul. It was at that point that I decided I was going to do whatever it took to show him I meant it, even if he yelled at me, gave me the cold shoulder, or was unreasonable. I do love the guy after all, and I really wanted it to work!"

Full Responsibility for the Relationship's Impact on its Environment

Taking full responsibility for the relationship's impact on its wider environment involves recognizing that the relationship exists in a broader system. It requires that each partner take responsibility for their relationship's impacts on the wider system in which it exists (e.g., home, community, work) and the people who reside there (e.g., children, family members, friends). This requires making the necessary adjustments when the relationship's actual impact doesn't align with each partner's desired impact or with their professed values (e.g., I'm angry at my wife for cheating on me. I've been expressing my anger and taking it out on her. Because of this, our house is a tense place right now, and not the environment that I want our kids to grow up in. I won't pretend I'm not angry, but I'm going to work on finding another way of expressing it so that my kids don't suffer.). Failing to do this opens the way for blame, victimhood, and disconnection to shape the relationship.

Responsibility and Infidelity

For a couple to heal from infidelity, both partners must learn to take full responsibility in all four dimensions. Otherwise, outstanding issues and hurts will be inadequately addressed and repaired. Without partners taking full responsibility, it's likely that these issues, or new ones, will reoccur and compound existing damage to their relationship.

However, taking full responsibility is a skill that can only be practiced when a person is in their wise adult. Adaptive children, by nature, are incapable of taking any kind of responsibility since their fundamental stance is anti-relational.

As partners work through the infidelity recovery process, complete trauma work, and become familiar with their wise adult, you can teach them how to use the skills involved in taking full responsibility. Practicing these skills, while receiving your coaching and feedback, can help them 1) work through ongoing issues, 2) repair unintended hurts, and 3) move towards creating a healthier, more intimate relationship based on trust. This is trust that the relationship is valued and shared equally and fully by both partners, as well as trust that both partners are invested and engaged enough to take whatever steps are necessary for repair to occur when conflict arises, and missteps occur. The following story explores the nuances of this.

"What really struck me early on in our repair process," Emelia discloses, *"is how much my friends were willing to throw Bob under the bus by blaming him for my affair. At first, it felt validating and empowering. I wasn't the one in the wrong. He was! Listening to them also made it so much easier to feel like a victim. I began to feel like I had no choice but to have an affair to get my needs met. In fact, I felt downright righteous.*

"However, once I realized I didn't want our relationship to end and that I was committed to staying in it, or at least staying long enough to see if we could salvage our relationship, things began to change. As we started to move forward and sort out the mess we were in, I realized that blaming Bob was disempowering for me. Feeling like I didn't have any choice in the matter actually felt bad. It didn't feel honest or authentic either. I now know this is very important to me, given that authenticity is one of my core values.

"As I saw Bob step in and acknowledge some of the areas in which he'd failed, like turning towards work instead of towards me for

connection and purpose, I began to see the areas I could take responsibility for. If I had been more honest with myself, and with him, we might not have gotten to that place of disconnection. As we both began to be more honest about our thoughts and feelings, it seemed to become easier for both of us to take responsibility for ourselves and the impact we'd had on each other and on our relationship.

"That's when I started to realize the impact our relationship had had on our friend circle: Many of our friends felt like they had to take sides to show that they were loyal and caring. Eventually, when both of us spoke to our friends, we let them know we wouldn't be burdening them with our problems anymore and that, if we slipped, we didn't expect them to take sides. We wanted them to be there equally for both of us — and our relationship!"

Awareness

A relationship contains more than just the people within it. It contains feelings, behaviors, moods, energy, content, perspective, tension/pressures, and context. Awareness refers to each partner's ability to be attuned to what's going on in their relationship's ecosystem, and to the signs that provide them with clues. Feelings of discomfort, for example, can indicate a values violation or that a person is moving away from one of their core values. Alternatively, a partner who notices that they aren't speaking as much with their partner, or that they're not spending as much time together, is provided with a signal that the distance between the two of them is growing.

Awareness and Infidelity

By teaching partners awareness skills, you help them notice when they're closer to the relationship they desire or moving farther away from it. Having these cues encourages them to step in and provide remediation and/or address issues that may be festering, before they escalate or morph into ones that are more difficult to resolve. All of this serves to increase their intimacy on an ongoing basis and creates the conditions that helps protect the relationship against the risk of further infidelity. The following story illustrates how this skill can be cultivated and strengthened.

"These days," Bob exclaims, "we're like a well-oiled machine. We each check in regularly with ourselves and with each other and make a point of connecting at the end of the day, even if, on a busy day, it's only for 20 minutes to share what's going on. This check-in helps both of us communicate any misgivings, concerns, or feelings we might be having that could, if ignored, fester into a bigger issue that we might have to deal with later. Even if we can't resolve the problem, it sets the ball in motion.

"At first, I was quite reluctant to participate in this structured check-in. It felt like a chore and kind of artificial — I felt like if I didn't come up with something, I wasn't being in touch enough and failing a test. Over time, though, I have to admit, these check-ins have become one of my favorite parts of the day.

"I don't always have something I want to share, and neither does Emelia, but I always notice that I feel more connected to her afterwards. Sometimes, I even learn something new about her, something I didn't think was possible after all these years. It's really given me a new perspective on the idea that you can grow old with someone and still never know them completely. Our relationship still has its ups and downs, but these days, I always feel like we'll be able to work out any problems we have together and get to a better place."

STCI

STCI (pronounced "sticky") stands for Stop, Think, Choose, Implement. Mastering and applying these four skills is critical for resolving conflicts, whether the issue being dealt with occurred in the past or is unfolding in the present.

Stop

"Stop" refers to a person stopping what they're doing, saying, and thinking. The objective is for a partner to stop focusing on their internal monologue, the one that's driving their actions, to refocus their attention on what's happening in the present, and to calm their nervous system so they can reregulate. Stopping involves a person listening to their partner and becoming aware of what's happening in their relational biosphere. If nothing else, performing this step stops a conflict from escalating. Often, this step alone can change an interaction's trajectory and shift its outcome in a more positive direction.

Think

"Think" requires that a person: 1) think about what they're doing, 2) think about their ideas, feelings, and behaviors, 3) think about what they're hearing and observing, and 4) think about their personal and relationship values (including their desired goals and outcomes). Finally, it involves thinking about the available options (individual and in partnership) as next steps. Each person may think about all of this on their own or aloud with their partner.

Choose

"Choose" involves a person choosing the thoughts and ideas that they will pursue. This may involve cycling back and forth to the thinking stage before finally deciding. A person can choose on their own or in partnership. In a solo choice, a person may, for example, decide to react to their partner with compassion and curiosity instead of anger. In a partnered choice, all partners may choose to discuss the issue at a later date, or they may choose a new and different course of action to address a key relationship need or goal.

Implement

After making a choice, the next step is to implement it. Here, the goal is to execute the chosen course of action, be it small (e.g., an attitudinal shift) or large (e.g., deciding to change course and move forward together).

STCI involves ongoing monitoring and assessing of the choice's impact (i.e., whether it's bringing us closer to our partner and our goals or further away from them). Implementation isn't the STCI process's last stage, but rather an active step that requires having a willingness to either do more of the choice, if it's having the desired impact, or pivoting and reengaging to make a different choice.

STCI and Infidelity

STCI is a self-regulation tool partners can use when they feel themselves becoming reactive or when they feel their adaptive child is emerging. It's also a tool that helps partners take full responsibility (in all four spheres) and become more relational. Teaching couples in infidelity recovery how to use this tool at the outset of the repair process helps them remain in their wise adult as they navigate issues and uncomfortable feelings that arise. Using STCI also encourages them to take full ownership for their relationship's well-being and to work towards improving it. The following story demonstrates how a couple can use this tool to change their communication dynamic and build intimacy.

"In the beginning, I'd notice myself getting furious with Emelia whenever she started talking about why she'd had an affair and what it did for her," Bob says. "It was like I couldn't contain myself. Hearing she was remorseful but that she also got some positives out of it made me feel like more of a failure — as a husband and as a man. And then, that insecure part of me would just let loose in ways that were really unhealthy for our relationship.

"Eventually, I realized my responses weren't helping and I decided to stop getting furious and start getting curious. I promised myself that next time Emelia talked, I'd just listen — not just stop talking and give her airtime, but really listen to what she had to say.

"I won't pretend it was easy. It was hard, really hard, to do. And, although painful, it really helped me realize how I'd boxed Emelia into a corner, leaving her with very little choice. Once I realized that, it became easier to think about interacting differently with Emelia and then actually doing it. I was shocked by how well she responded. My choosing to do something different and her different response wound up accelerating our ability to look at what wasn't working for us as a couple and trying on new behaviors and ways of being until we found ones that worked better for us."

The Four Relationship Cornerstones

The CHI Relationship Map's four relationship cornerstones (commit to what is, communicate heart truth, be curious, and be open to possibilities) are skills and reliable tools that provide partners with sustenance, clarity, and a strategy when they're navigating conflict. When applied, they help partners navigate conflict in a relational manner and, in peaceful times, they help each person gain deeper insight into their relationship and their partner.

Partners who aren't in relational harmony can retreat to any of the CHI Relationship Map's corners, as in a wrestling ring, for respite. There, they can calm their inner landscape and retool. When they're ready to reemerge, they can reengage using one of the relationship cornerstones to obtain a deeper understanding and move forward based on their wise adult's vision of the end goals.

Commit to What Is

"Commit to what is" refers to the idea of committing to the current situation, the situation as it exists, not as a person wishes it were or believes it should be. Committing to what is means focusing on the present, not on the past, while avoiding engaging in blame or shifting into a mythical future.

Making this commitment involves recognizing that the past can't be changed, that the future is yet to be written, and that only by staying in the present and dealing with the current situation can each person influence the shape of what is yet to come. It requires that each partner show up authentically, meaningfully, and sometimes vulnerably, without judgment, while fully acknowledging all feelings that are present.

Committing to What Is and Infidelity

By teaching this skill to both partners at the outset of the infidelity recovery process, you help them both stay in the here and now. As each partner masters this skill and learns to focus on what is, the amount of blame thrown about is reduced. A partner (especially the hurt partner) who commits to what is increases their chance of being heard by the other person. Counterintuitively, it also typically increases the likelihood that they get the outcome they desire. The following illustrates how this unfolds.

"When I first found out about Emelia's infidelity, I went through the roof!" Bob recalls. "I was enraged, and I kept wishing we could go back to before — before I knew about her infidelity, before I realized our marriage had cracks in it, before I realized that Emelia was capable of cheating on me and putting our relationship at risk. For a long time, I'd alternate between thinking about what she should have done — which was obviously not to be with someone else — and what I could have done differently. All of this kept me in the past, unable to face the situation we were in.

"It was only after I accepted that it had happened, and that this was our starting point for moving forward, that we were able to get traction in terms of changing our relationship. I truly think that until I could accept this as our reality, I wasn't able to engage — I was stuck in an alternate reality that I constantly created and recreated in my mind."

Communicate Heart Truth

Communicating heart truth requires that a person speak from their heart, not from their head. It doesn't mean avoiding an issue or conflict. Instead, it means that a partner addresses the issue or conflict by speaking about their desires, wants, and needs in a non-blaming and nonjudgmental way. It typically involves using many "I" statements to express a range of thoughts and feelings and using more nonviolent communication tools beyond simply providing and receiving feedback.

Unlike typically rigid head truth, which is often judgmental and filled with black-and-white thinking (the adaptive child's go-to place), heart truth is more vulnerable. Heart truth allows a person to articulate their feelings, wants, needs, and hurts. With heart truth, a person can address the impact an action or behavior had on them without blaming and judging the other person, something that typically pushes them away.

Speaking heart truth allows a person to be simultaneously strong and soft and to connect with the person they love without needing to avoid hard truths. Teaching partners how to do this allows the recovery process to unfold while ensuring that underlying issues won't be avoided or remain unresolved.

Communicating Heart Truth and Infidelity

Communicating heart truth, rather than head truth, is a skill that, when mastered, can significantly help couples in the process of repairing from infidelity. It lets both partners speak their truth, be heard, and create a bridge on which to walk side by side as they build a better future for themselves. Teaching this skill to your couple in the first RLT phase helps them transition more smoothly and impactfully through subsequent phases and improves their overall ability to act in a relational manner. The following demonstrates how this works.

"I remember the first time I spoke my heart truth to Emelia. It was early on, and I was still in shock at discovering her betrayal. I was also enraged. We had just started therapy and what I wanted to do was scream at her and tell her how awful she was as a person.

"After working with our therapist, I was able to take a different track and tell Emelia, 'Honey, I'm really angry with you. You betrayed our marriage vows, and you kept secrets from me for a long time. I feel like a laughingstock when I think about the fact that some of our friends knew what you were up to before I did. I'm also really hurt because I feel like I can't trust you or the stability of our marriage anymore. And I want to. I want to know that I can trust you not to cheat on me again and that I can rely on you to be truthful. I want to work with you to figure out how we can make this happen. And I'm scared.'

"At first, talking like this felt totally unnatural and corny, but after seeing Emelia's defenses melt a bit and seeing that she wasn't going to counterattack, I realized that there might be some validity to this heart-truth thing."

Be Curious

Many people find it hard to stay in their wise adult in the face of a triggering event. Conflicts or triggering events quickly push their wise adult aside, bringing their adaptive child to the fore. When this happens, a person rapidly and almost imperceptibly makes assumptions. They're ready to take everything personally and respond to the personal "attack" by using one or all of their losing relational strategies, each of which was forged in their past as a dysfunctional means to ensure their survival.

RLT teaches people to take a time out when they're triggered. The idea is to use the time out as a space to reconnect with their wise adult and to recenter so that when they come back to their partner, they're more capable of interacting in a relationally positive manner. However, as Einstein posited, the same mindset that created a problem will never be able to solve it. Returning to the same conditions that originally triggered the emergence of their adaptive child without having different strategies in place stacks the odds in favor of their adaptive child reemerging.

Being curious is a strategy a person can use to mitigate the likelihood of their adaptive child reemerging. Remembering to be curious — curious about their assumptions, curious about the meaning they're attributing to what the other person is saying and doing, curious about their own emotions and reactions — can be a game changer. It can shift their mental and emotional landscape from one in which only black and white exist to one where many shades of gray reside.

Partners who act on their curiosity reduce the likelihood that their, or their partner's, anger and blame will escalate. When curiosity is front and center, doors to deeper conversations open and partners can be more vulnerable, transparent, and clear. All of this helps reduce the overall conflict levels. It also creates the conditions in which each partner can develop a deeper understanding of each other's wants, needs, fears, hopes, and desires.

Curiosity and Infidelity

Fostering a climate based on mutual respect where deep listening occurs makes it more likely that true intimacy will emerge. By teaching the involved and the hurt partner to develop and use their curiosity throughout each RLT phase, you ensure that partners learn to better listen to one another. Accessing their curiosity also helps them stay in their wise adult for longer periods of time, even when blame and judgment show up. And, once curiosity becomes embedded in a relationship's fabric, it contributes to a greater possibility that long-term relational transformation will occur and that both partners will experience relational satisfaction. The following story explores curiosity's impact on a relationship.

"For a long time, I was convinced that I was right and that I had the full picture of how we had gotten to a place where I was not only willing, but also eager to cheat on Bob," Emelia recounts. "Of course, in my mind, it was mostly his fault, which made me feel righteous and defensive when he tried to talk with me.

"Slowly, though, the more I heard Bob, the less sure I became that I was right. I started to get curious about my assumptions as to why Bob was spending so much time at work and not interacting with me in the evenings, rebuffing me when I wanted to get closer. Curiosity prompted me to ask him some questions — not just to get information that I could use to support my point of view, but to genuinely find out what had made him change so drastically from the man I used to know and had fallen in love with.

"Finding out that Bob felt a lot of pressure to move up the ranks at work and get some promotions before we had kids was a huge surprise for me. I hadn't realized that he wanted to make sure that we were provided for and that he wanted to make sure that he was in a position to have more flexibility once our first baby was born precisely because he wanted to spend more time with us. I never realized that it was important for him to do this since we had agreed early on that I would be the one to stay home with our kids.

"It blew my mind to realize how wrong I had gotten things and that Bob was spending so much time away from me and was so exhausted precisely because he wanted to be connected to me and his soon-to-be kids. I wondered what else I'd gotten wrong. That's when my curiosity really took root, and I was able to hear his answers to my questions. It helped me see Bob in an entirely new light and made me want to do the work to move forward. Now, I try not to assume anything, and our relationship has never been better!"

Be Open to Possibilities

Since adaptive children like to think in black and white, right and wrong, and other absolutes, they're often unable to consider other alternatives and possibilities, much less explore them. The final cornerstone, be open to possibilities, is a skill each partner can cultivate. When used, it helps keep their wise adult front and center.

Being open to possibilities requires that a person be open to the possibility that they may be wrong about their assumptions regarding what someone else is thinking, their motivations, what they're trying to communicate, what they're trying to accomplish, and the end results they're pursuing. When a partner is open to these unknowns, they're more capable of accessing and using their curiosity. As they become more open, new possibilities that may not have previously existed or been conceptualized emerge.

Being Open to Possibility and Infidelity

When dealing with infidelity, helping each partner develop the skill of being open to possibilities allows both the involved partner and the hurt partner to challenge their assumptions about themselves, their partner, and their relationship. As they do this, they're more likely to move from fixed positions to more malleable ones where they can, together, identify new possibilities for their relationship, possibilities that may ultimately invigorate it. The following demonstrates how this can occur.

"The more I got curious, the more I learned things about Bob that I never would have guessed. I learned he really wanted a family and that, deep down, he wanted it to be different from the family he grew up in. Unlike his dad, he wants to be close to his kids and be present, not just for the big milestones but for the mundane, everyday activities too.

"I learned he actually likes cooking and wanted to get better at it because it's fun and a great way to connect with people. He admitted there's nothing he loves more than having a busy house and a table full of people he cares about sharing a meal, especially a meal he's made for

them. It makes him feel like he's sharing himself and having fun at the same time.

"If we hadn't started talking, I never would have guessed any of this. What was also interesting to me was that, as Bob started sharing with me, I started to get curious about myself. The more curious I got, the more questions I had about myself. In the end, I started questioning some of my assumptions about motherhood and marriage. As I explored these, alone and with Bob, I realized I didn't want to be a full-time mom and that, on a certain level, I was dreading it. I realized what I truly craved was to be doing something on a regular basis that involved creativity.

"It was at this point that we both got curious about our assumptions regarding what marriage and family should look like, and everything became open for examination. As we explored options, we both realized we'd both be happier if I went back to work and Bob became the primary caregiver. It was a revelation for both of us, one that upended both of our long-held assumptions and made us, and our kids, happier in the end."

Relationship Stake

A relationship stake is a tool that helps partners keep their relationship front and center by maintaining a focus on what's in it for we (as opposed to what's in it for me). When used, it helps partners self-regulate and stay in their wise adult.

A relationship stake is not itself a purpose or an end goal. Rather, it's a statement that reflects what's important to both partners, a reminder of what they're in service of, and what they're both willing to go to the mat for when the unexpected arises. When partners support their relationship stake, and act in alignment with it, individual and relationship values are typically honored. Consequently, partners tend to move towards one another, frequently creating greater intimacy and joy within the relationship.

Both partners co-create a relationship stake. It can be literal and easy to understand (e.g., transparency above all else) or nuanced and opaque, with little meaning for anyone else (e.g., vibrant red fun intimacy). No matter what its form, it's a shorthand for the couple's focus, one that both agree on and buy into. Because the relationship stake is co-created and agreed upon, it's more likely that each person will make a choice that serves the relationship, not just a convenient or self-serving choice when faced with difficult situations (e.g., declining an invitation to a one-on-one after-work drink with an attractive co-worker).

A relationship stake is time or event bound — it has a beginning, middle, and end. It doesn't last forever and can be renegotiated or redesigned if no longer serving its intended purpose. It's also nonexclusive: a couple can create and maintain several concurrent stakes, each for a different purpose or intention. However, every relationship stake must be attainable, something that partners can lean into and bring to life through their thoughts, feelings, and behaviors.

Ultimately, a relationship stake provides each partner with a lens through which they can view and respond to events. It also gives them an anchor that they can hold on to when they find themselves adrift.

When used, this tool helps keep partners out of their adaptive child and in their wise adult. A concrete simple phrase that reminds them of what's important in any given situation, event, or time frame allows each partner to pause, recenter, and respond from a new vantage point. This vantage point is one that encourages them to check their unfolding assumptions and not take personally what's being said or done.

It also helps partners stay 1) out of grandiosity, a position from which most entitled actions detrimental to a relationship occur, and 2) in the circle of health, the only place positive relationality is possible. All of this is important for partners who are designing a new type of relationship based on intimacy, respect, and connection and practicing behaviors that bring that relationship to life.

Relationship Stake and Infidelity

By teaching your clients how to create and use a relationship stake, you set the groundwork for them to not only create common goals but also to create a relationship that focuses on both partners' needs, wants, and desires, all while being able to navigate conflictual and uncomfortable situations with aplomb and a sense of togetherness. The story explores how this can take place.

"Emelia and I really love using relationship stakes whenever we're planning a big event, or even just to deal with ongoing stresses. At first, we thought the idea was a little hokey and weird. But after we created one and used it, we were sold!" Bob proclaims.

"Yup," Emilia chimes in. "The first time we created one, we couldn't quite see the purpose of it but decided to give it a go anyways. We were having my family and Bob's family over for Christmas dinner for the first time after my affair. They ALL knew all about my affair, and we knew all about their opinions and were sure the dinner was going to be uncomfortable and tense. We had also just found out I was pregnant and wanted to tell everyone at the same time. We both weren't sure how that was going to go. It was pretty nerve-racking.

"So, Bob and I sat down and talked about what we would ideally like to happen, both in terms of the outcome and in terms of how we'd feel throughout the event. Some of the things that came up were connection, joy, acceptance, and equanimity. In the end, we came up with a relationship stake of 'pink hearts gliding easily.' We decided we would say the whole thing or parts of it to ourselves and each other if we found ourselves getting reactive or wanting to act in ways that wouldn't bring us closer to connection, joy, acceptance, and equanimity."

"It was super helpful," Bob recalls, "especially before we told them about the baby. My mother was making snide remarks to Emelia. Emelia wasn't that reactive, but I could feel that I was starting to get my hackles up. Emelia noticed and walked by me and said, 'glide easily.' It made me remember not to sweat the little stuff and that we had much bigger things to put forward, things that would turn everyone's hearts pink.

"There were little moments like that the whole night long. Using the relationship stake, we were each able to help each other, and ourselves, stay on track, heading to where we wanted to be. It was pretty magical. Since then, we've created a lot of relationship stakes for a lot of different situations!"

Summary

The point at which one partner decides to engage in infidelity is a crossroads that influences a relationship's trajectory, as is how each partner chooses to navigate its aftermath. Just as relational demise isn't infidelity's foregone conclusion, neither is relational transformation.

A couple can use an experience of infidelity as an inspiration to gain deeper insight into their relationship (and each other). They can then use this knowledge to design a renewed relationship founded on greater intimacy and relational joy. Their chances of success in this endeavor, however, are greatly increased when helped by a couples therapist equipped with a stalwart theoretical approach to guide them through this process. RLT provides such an approach.

As a therapist, you can address RLT's limitations by incorporating the CHI Relationship Map and its tools into the RLT process and teaching them to your clients. Overlaying the CHI Relationship Map onto RLT's approach to post-infidelity repair is more likely to effect a positive outcome for couples in that they move towards living in the circle of health. This is a place where they interact with one another, for the most part, from their wise adult and in a relational manner that gives birth to a deep sense of knowing, curiosity, and intimacy, all of which form the waters in which they swim.

TL;DR

- RLT's approach to post-infidelity repair and transformation is **flexible** enough to incorporate other tools to help address its limitations.

- The **CHI Relationship Map and its six tools**, when used, allow people to 1) recognize when they're moving farther away from one another, 2) stay in their wise adult, 3) resolve conflicts more relationally, and 4) move towards one another to meet co-created relationship goals, including ones geared towards creating a relationship based on monogamy, trust, and intimacy.

- **Boundaries** are important for any intimate relationship. A relationship's boundaries are composed of two elements: 1) a commitment to stay in relationship with our partner when difficulties arise, and 2) individual and relationship values. When values are transgressed, a relationship can recover if appropriate repair takes place. Often, effective repair leads to a stronger relationship based on deeper understanding and commitment. A strong relationship boundary provides an effective bulwark against infidelity.

- Each person in a relationship is **100% responsible** for 1) their own actions, thoughts, and feelings, 2) their impact on the other person(s) in the relationship, 3) the relationship itself, and 4) their relationship's impact on the broader environment in which it resides.

- **Full responsibility** isn't the same as blame; it means owning our choices and their impacts and doing whatever is needed to address a resulting problem or create improvement in our relationship. When partners are able to take full responsibility, it deepens the post-infidelity repair process. It also allows partners to work through ongoing issues, repair unintended hurts, and move towards creating a healthier, more intimate relationship based on trust.

- Cultivating the ability to attune to our relationship's ecosystem allows us to develop **awareness** when something is out of alignment. Partners who are skilled at this are quickly aware when something is out of alignment in their relationship. This allows them to intervene early and prevents 1) issues from escalating, and 2) infidelity from becoming an attractive solution to disconnection and discontent.

- **STCI (Stop, Think, Choose, Implement)** is a four-step iterative skill-based process that, when used, can help resolve conflicts and prevent escalation. Using this tool helps keep partners in their wise adult and helps them take full responsibility and be more relational. When dealing with infidelity, it encourages both partners to take full ownership of their relationship's well-being.

- The **four relationship cornerstones** (commit to what is, communicate heart truth, be curious, and be open to possibilities) are skills and tools that partners can rely on for sustenance, clarity, and strategy when navigating a conflict. They encourage navigating conflict more relationally and, in times of peace, help partners develop deeper insight into each other and their relationship. When utilized, they help keep each person in their wise adult. When applied to the post-infidelity repair process, they help each partner achieve a greater understanding of the events that led up to the infidelity, resolve past hurts and grievances, and create a more fulfilling relationship that they can step into as they move forward together.

- Partners can use a **relationship stake** to help each other keep their gaze on what's important for the relationship. Using a relationship stake can help both partners remain in their wise adult, especially when designing a new relationship post-infidelity.

"Live as if you were to die tomorrow. Learn as if you were to live forever."

—Mahatma Gandhi

"Don't brood. Get on with living and loving. You don't have forever."

—Leo Buscaglia

"We all die. The goal isn't to live forever, the goal is to create something that will."

—Chuck Palahniuk

Chapter 8

So, What Now?

"I know that we're making our journey seems relatively straightforward," Emelia reflects, *"and it was anything but."*

"Yeah," Bob says. *"For the first eight months after Emelia's infidelity came to light, I wasn't even sure that we would be living in the same house the following week. I was alternately furious with Emelia, wanting to get rid of her as quickly as possible and punish her in the most excruciating fashion in the process, and desperate to make things work while having guarantees that she'd never again look at another man. I wouldn't say I was exactly rational. In fact, I'd say that it took me a long time to know what I wanted to do with our relationship and the direction I wanted it to move towards. It took me even longer to take some responsibility around my role in getting our relationship to the state it was in."*

"Same for me. When Bob initially found out about my affair, I was so invested in the idea that my affair was Bob's fault and that he had driven me to it that I was unable to take any responsibility for my decisions and actions. It was only through ongoing discussions with our therapist that I was able to start to see that I was responsible, at least in part, for what had happened to our marriage and that it wasn't all on Bob's shoulders. It wasn't long after that I came to the realization that if I wanted things to be different, I had to behave in different, more relational ways. I also realized that if I didn't know how to do so, I had to take the initiative to learn."

"Yes," Bob chimes in. "Our therapist was instrumental in helping both of us see that we weren't merely victims, subject to the other person's whims and the vagaries of our relationship. She helped us see that we both have agency. At least that's how I saw it."

"Absolutely!" Emelia exclaims. "Before therapy, I never understood that I could create, and co-create, my relationships. It was only through our therapeutic sessions that I came to realize that not only do I have that power but that assuming it, albeit a scary undertaking, is what would allow me to have the kind of relationship I truly want. For me, this was a revelation. It helped me understand that I had this power all along and that my acting out by having an affair was, in fact, a way of giving up my power."

"I also felt more agency as we went through the process," Bob shares. "The more I understood what was important to Emelia, and to myself, and the assumptions we both had made along the way, the more I was able to see that, moving forward, I could make more informed choices, ones that are more in line with what I value and want to create. The fact that our therapist never seemed to doubt that we could both learn to take responsibility for our past decisions and for creating our future was also really important to me — it gave me something to hold on to whenever I felt like our situation was hopeless."

"I agree," Emelia says. "Our therapist's belief that we were both capable of so much more — not because we were broken or fatally flawed, but because we are imperfect, learning human beings — also gave me hope. Her belief in us made me feel like our possibilities were infinite — or at least much more than the obvious choices of splitting up or biting our tongues and returning to our old status quo. You know, the horribly conflictual one we were locked into when we started therapy."

"I also felt like our therapist was our cheerleader — rooting for us, without pressuring us to choose a specific course of action or pressuring us with a specific time frame in which we needed to make a decision about our relationship. I felt like she was invested in us, invested in our well-being, and willing to support us in whatever way we needed, without creating a pressurized environment that required us to move *at a particular pace or towards a specific goal. I think this spaciousness helped me feel like I could take my time to process my emotions and figure out what I really wanted and what I was truly ready to commit to," Bob adds.*

"I agree," Emilia chimes in. "Our therapist's curiosity, which was always present without an obvious attachment to a specific outcome that we needed to decide on, allowed our curiosity — about ourselves, each other, and our relationship — to bloom. I'd say that this skill, one we were both pretty unskilled at, is one of the factors that allowed us to find a way back to each other after my infidelity. I also believe it's a critical factor in our ongoing success."

Successful relationships are flexible and adapt to changes that inevitably arise over the course of a long-term partnership. Partners who wholeheartedly and continuously engage in the work required to complete the cycle of connection, disconnection, and reconnection as they face inevitable relational betrayals are more likely to remain committed and fulfilled throughout it all.

Infidelity, however, is a specific type of betrayal. When a couple suffers from infidelity, disconnection is often a contributory cause and almost always a subsequent result. Consequently, many partners find it hard to work through infidelity's aftermath and reconnect.

In fact, for many couples, infidelity is a showstopper. The relationship either ends, or the partners stay together, living much as they did previously, but with the added layers of anger and mistrust permeating their relationship.

Only couples who've successfully completed the cycle of harmony, disharmony, and post-infidelity repair can break the chains of anger, recriminations, and despair. Some couples who achieve this are also able to transform their relationship into one that's more collaborative, connected, and greater than the sum of its parts. Most couples need help to be successful in this undertaking.

As a therapist, this is where you come in. This chapter focuses on three high-level skills and perspectives you can apply, both to yourself and to your post-infidelity clients, to increase their (and your) odds of success.

Everyone Is Fully Responsible and Fully Capable

When infidelity occurs, it's easy for the hurt partner to move into blame and find fault with the other person, or even themself. When this happens, it becomes even easier for the hurt partner to get stuck. The involved partner may also be stuck in terms of feeling angry, victimized, resentful, retaliatory, ashamed, and guilty. As a therapist, you can help your clients process their thoughts and emotions, so they move through them and approach their partner from their wise adult and with a more open heart.

Once this occurs, it's easier for each partner to take ownership of their thoughts and emotions and see how they might be responsible for the infidelity and for the current state of their relationship. This responsibility may include taking responsibility for past actions, emotions, and thoughts that contributed to the infidelity, or ones that contribute to disharmony and distance in the present. It may also include taking responsibility for changes needed to create the future they want for themselves and their relationship as they move forward.

Taking responsibility reduces each person's desire and ability to lay blame on the other and increases their willingness to engage in actions geared towards improving the situation and their relationship. It fosters a mindset and a desire to communicate in ways that not only don't hurt their partner, or their relationship, but also build it up.

Each partner may go through the process of taking responsibility at a different pace. Viewing each person as naturally creative, resourceful, and whole allows you to hold each person as fully responsible and fully capable. Adopting this perspective, in turn, allows you to encourage and support them in this process, without feeling pressured about timelines, or pressured to intervene to obtain a specific goal. Effectively, being able to stay steadfast in this perspective raises the odds that each partner will eventually take responsibility on their own accord and make the changes necessary to not only repair their relationship, but also transform it into one that's more relational, satisfying, and inspiring.

Curiosity Is Key

The adage that curiosity killed the cat points to a belief that sometimes permeates therapy, especially when dealing with post-infidelity recovery. A therapist, for example, may be hesitant to explore what the involved partner gained from the infidelity or what they will miss about the relationship for fear of alienating the hurt partner, making them angry, escalating a current conflict, or causing more damage to the relationship. Although these risks are real, engaging curiosity while holding each partner as fully capable and responsible may, in fact, be the key that allows the couple to free themselves from the assumptions, perspectives, and misunderstandings that are imprisoning them in their current pattern.

As humans, we all make assumptions about ourselves, our partners, our roles, how our relationships and the world should be organized, and what's possible. Because we don't often talk about these assumptions, or even question them, we tend to assume that others hold the same assumptions we do. This is particularly problematic in relationships, and even more so when in an intimate relationship. Not only do our assumptions box us in and limit our options, but they also curtail our ability to grow and change. This is particularly true when dealing with the often-competing beliefs and emotions associated with post-infidelity.

Curiosity allows us to ask questions that challenge our assumptions, foster understanding, and potentially lay our fears to rest. When employed with an open heart, curiosity allows partners to ask each other where they are coming from (e.g., the values, thoughts, and feelings that influenced their behaviors or decisions), where they are in the present (e.g., angry, sad, guilty, remorseful, frustrated, hopeful, connected, disconnected), and where they'd like to be in the future.

Essentially, employing curiosity allows partners to be open to new and different interpretations, thoughts, and ideas and to receive information without overlaying their judgments, fears, or assumptions on it. It also makes the process of identifying each person's needs, preferences, and desires less fraught. This, in turn, allows each person to develop a more precise and accurate picture of what's going on, not just for themselves but for everyone involved.

Ultimately, operating from a place of curiosity makes the relationship safer, lowers defenses, and opens hearts. For partners knee-deep in post-infidelity repair, tapping into their curiosity provides a key to exit the murky bog in which they find themselves and expands what's possible. As the therapist, you can help the partners access their curiosity by asking questions about issues previously glossed over or avoided and by modeling an openhearted, nonjudgmental, and engaged response to what shows up.

By maintaining your own curiosity about the people in front of you, and their relationship, you're also less likely to be biased towards one person or a specific outcome. You're more likely to accept and effectively engage with whatever shows up, all while adhering to the belief that connection and transformation are possible. By maintaining this attitude and engagement, you further act in service of the couple by continuously providing them with hope that their story can have a better ending.

Let Go of Outcome

As a therapist, you may find it easy to root for your couple and their happy ending or even become invested in a certain outcome. The same may hold true for one or more of the partners.

Helping partners to focus on the present, including the fact that infidelity has occurred and a rupture exists makes it easier for them, and you, to fully and openheartedly engage with whatever shows up in the here and now. Focusing on the present, in turn, makes it easier for partners to authentically and transparently show up for one another without agenda or blame. This creates a meaningful experience in which each partner develops an awareness that they matter and that they have the power to choose and create.

It also makes it easier for them to let go of the past, and to let go of specific events they might wish had been different. Once they've done so, you can help them focus on questions such as "What's needed *now*? Where do we want to go *now*? What are our next steps *now*?"

Ultimately, by helping partners focus on the present, you help them develop a greater chance that they will create the future they desire.

Letting go of outcome and focusing on the present also makes it easier for you, as the therapist, to hold your clients to be fully responsible and capable and to let go of your own desired outcome for them. Adopting this stance makes it easier for you to be wholly present for your couple and provide them with what's needed in the moment. This, in turn, creates space for whatever needs to emerge and for an unscripted outcome (whether they stay together or not) that meets both partners' needs to evolve.

Concluding Thoughts

Dealing with post-infidelity repair can be tricky for a couples therapist. The path towards repair and transformation isn't a straightforward one, and it often follows a two steps forward and one step back trajectory. Throughout this process, emotions run high, the unexpected shows up, partners' doubts creep in, and their commitment to the process and to the relationship waxes and wanes.

When working with partners to repair their relationship post-infidelity and to transform it into something more relational, it's helpful to not only keep in mind the importance of good relationships and their consequence for our health, happiness, and overall well-being, but to also communicate this to them, again and again. Emphasizing this while reminding them of their own relationship's value can help them stay with, and engaged in, this difficult and often heartrending process.

Ultimately, for this process of repair and transformation to be successful, the therapist needs to have patience, perspective, skills, tools, and a roadmap. Applying RLT, the CHI Relationship Map, and its associated tools lightens your burden, making it easier to focus on what's required in the here and now, all while tracking and mapping the couple's progress against a broader chart. This is key to helping your clients find their way back to one another and to helping them create a relationship that's based on shared values, honesty, clear commitment, deep engagement, a willingness to be vulnerable, and shared partnership. In essence, if they choose to stay together, adopting this process allows you to help them create a relationship that's nurturing and fulfilling, one they're both passionate about.

Glossary of Terms

Adaptive child: According to RLT, the adaptive child is the part of each person that was forged after the age of five due to relational trauma. The adaptive child is a child's version of an adult and tends to think in black-and-white terms and be perfectionistic, relentless, rigid, harsh, certain, and hard, while living in a body that is tight/tense.

Attachment style: The bonding pattern that children learn and bring, as adults, into their relationships.

Betrayal: A violation of a person's trust, confidence, expectation, agreement, or moral standard.

Blatant: An RLT term that refers to the relational partner who's more relationally dysfunctional and who frequently engages in boundary-violating and grandiose behaviors.

Characterological change: A change in a person's fundamental character.

Circle of health: An RLT term that refers to the place where someone operates as a wise adult and doesn't escape into shame or grandiosity, seeing themselves as equal to (not better or less than) the person with whom they are interacting.

First consciousness: An RLT term that refers to the knee jerk reaction a person has to their partner when they're operating out of their limbic system. It is typically associated with a fight, flight, freeze, or fawn response.

Grandiosity: A person's sense of entitlement that's frequently expressed in boundary-violating behaviors (e.g., yelling, controlling, retaliation), with little regard for the impact of their behavior on others.

Hurt partner: The person in the relationship who's betrayed and hurt by the infidelity.

Involved partner: The partner in the relationship who's committing infidelity.

Joining through the truth: An RLT term that refers to confronting a client with the truth about their bad behavior in such a way that they feel seen and understood.

Latent: An RLT term that refers to the partner with the least amount of power in the relationship.

Leverage: A partner's motivation for change.

Losing relational strategies: Relational strategies that, when employed, undermine intimacy and/or the relationship itself. According to RLT, there are five losing relational strategies: withdrawal, needing to be right, control, retaliation, and unbridled self-expression.

Psychological patriarchy: The belief that 1) humans can be divided into two halves based on masculine and feminine qualities, and 2) feminine qualities are worth less than masculine qualities (i.e., masculine qualities are typically exalted by the larger society).

Second consciousness: An RLT term that refers to a person who is operating out of their wise adult and who has access to their prefrontal cortex. This state is marked by an ability to self-regulate and interact in a relational manner.

Shame: A person's belief that they, as a person, are not good or worthy (i.e., there is something wrong with them at their core).

Stance-stance-dance: An RLT term used to reflect a relational dance that's composed of the relational stances adopted by each partner.

Transmission reception work: An RLT term that refers to work that's done with the latent so that they can receive the new, more relational behaviors that the blatant is engaging in.

Wise adult: An RLT term that refers to a person who can pause and refrain from using losing relational strategies when confronted or engaged in conflict and, instead, respond intentionally. Wise adults typically operate out of their prefrontal cortex and are defined by being nuanced, realistic, forgiving, flexible, warm, yielding, humble, and relaxed in their body.

References

Abrahamson, I., Hussain, R., Khan, A., & Schofield, M. J. (2011). What helps couples rebuild their relationship after infidelity? *Journal of Family Issues, 33*(11), 1494–1519. https://doi.org/10.1177/0192513X11424257

Abzug, R. (2016). Extramarital affairs as occupational hazard: A structural, ethical (cultural) model of opportunity. *Sexualities, 19*, 25–45.

Atkins, D. C., Baucom, D. H., & Jacobson, N. S. (2001). Understanding infidelity: Correlates in a national sample. *Journal of Family Psychology, 15*, 735–749.

Baruch, V. (n.d). Full respect living toolkit — The essentials of living relationally [PDF]. https://vivianbaruch.com/wp-content/uploads/2013/03/1.-What-is-Full-Respect-Living.pdf

Baucom, D. H., Gordon, K. C., Snyder, D. K., Atkins, D. C., & Christensen, A. (2006). Treating affair couples: Clinical considerations and initial findings. *Journal of Cognitive Psychotherapy, 20*(4), 375–392. https://doi.org/10.1891/jcpiq-v20i4a004

Blow, A. & Hartnett, K. (2005). Infidelity in committed relationships II: A substantive review. *Journal of Marital and Family Therapy, 31*(2), 217–233.

Brewer, G., Hunt, D., James, G., & Abell, L. (2015). Dark triad traits, infidelity and romantic revenge. *Personality and Individual Differences, 83*, 122–127.

Brooks, T. J., & Monaco, K. (2013) Your cheatin' heart: Joint production, joint consumption and the likelihood of extramarital sex. *Applied Economic Letters, 20*(3), 272–275. https://doi.org/10.1080/13504851.2012.690845

Browness, S. (2021, August 19). What is sexual desire discrepancy and how it affects your relationships [Blogpost]. *Bluehart.* https://www.blueheart.io/your-relationship

Burdette, A. M., Ellison, C. G., Sherkat, D. E., & Gore, K. A. (2007). Are there religious variations in marital infidelity? *Journal of Family Issues, 28*(12), 1553–1581. https://doi.org/10.1177/0192513X07304269

Burgo, J. (2013, May 30). The difference between guilt and shame. *Psychology Today.* https://www.psychologytoday.com/us/blog/shame/201305/the-difference-between-guilt-and-shame

Buscho, A. G. (2022, February 1). Is your marriage doomed after an affair? *Psychology Today.* https://www.psychologytoday.com/us/blog/better-divorce/202202/is-marriage-doomed-after-affair

Crysel, L. C., Crosier, B. S., & Webster, G. D. (2013). The dark triad and risk behavior. *Personality and Individual Differences, 54*(1), 35–40. https://doi.org/10.1016/j.paid.2012.07.029

Dating Scout. (2024, April). Ashley Madison review April 2024. *Dating Scout.* https://www.datingscout.com/ashley-madison/review

Didonato, T. E. (2019, October 18). The 8 main reasons why people cheat. *Psychology Today.* https://www.psychologytoday.com/us/blog/meet-catch-and-keep/201910/the-8-main-reasons-why-people-cheat

Dodgson, L. (2019, April 22). Ashley Madison now has 60 million users. Two men told us why they use it. *Business Insider.* https://www.businessinsider.com/why-men-use-ashley-madison-online-dating-2019-4

Drigotas, S. M., Safstrom, C. A., Gentilia, T. (1999). An investment model prediction of dating infidelity. *Journal of Personality and Social Psychology, 77*(3), 509–524. https://doi.org/10.1037/0022-3514.77.3.509

Ferrigan, M. M., Valentiner, D. P., & Berman, M. E. (2000). Psychopathy dimensions and awareness of negative and positive consequences of aggressive behavior in a nonforensic sample. *Personality and Individual Differences, 28*(3), 527–538.

Fincham, F., Paleari, F., & Regalia, C. (2002). Forgiveness in marriage: The role of relationship quality, attributions, and empathy. *Personal Relationships, 9*(10), 27–37.

Fuller, J. R. (n.d.). Infidelity and couple therapy outcomes. *New York Behavioral Health.* https://www.newyorkbehavioralhealth.com/infidelity-and-couple-therapy-outcomes/

Gaspard, T. (n.d.). Learning to love again after an affair. *Gottman Institute.* https://www.gottman.com/blog/learning-to-love-again-after-an-affair/

Glass, S. P. (2003). *NOT "just friends": Rebuilding trust and recovering your sanity after infidelity.* Free Press.

Gonzales-Rivera, J., Aquino-Serrano, F., & Perez-Torres, E. (2019). Relationship satisfaction and infidelity-related behaviors on social networks: A preliminary online study of Hispanic women. *European Journal Investigating Health Psychology Education, 10*(1), 297–309. https://www.ncbi.nlm.nih.gov/pmc/articles/PMC8314247/

Gordon, K. & Mitchell, E. (2020). Infidelity in the time of COVID-19. *Family Process, 9*(3), 956–966. doi: 10.1111/famp.12576

Gottman, J. & Silver, N. (2015). *The seven principles for making marriage work: A practical guide from the country's foremost relationship expert.* Harmony Books.

Guitar, A. E., Geher, G., Kruger, D. J., Garcia, J. R., Fisher, M. L., & Fitzgerald, C. J. (2016). Defining and distinguishing sexual and emotional infidelity. *Current Psychology, 36*, 434–446. https://doi.org/10.1007/s12144-016-9432-4

Hertlein, K. & Webster, M. (2008). Technology, relationships, and problems: A research synthesis. *Journal of Marital Family Therapy, 34*, 445–460. doi: 10.1111/j.1752-0606.2008.00087.x

Ilardi, S. (2009, July 13). Social isolation: A modern plague. *Psychology Today.* https://www.psychologytoday.com/intl/blog/the-depression-cure/200907/social-isolation-a-modern-plague

Janoff-Bulman, R. (1992). *Shattered assumptions: Towards a new psychology of trauma.* The Free Press.

Jeanfreau, M. M. & Mong, M. (2018). Barriers to marital infidelity. *Marriage and Family Review, 55*(1), 23–37. https://doi.org/10.1080/01494929.2018.1518821

Johnson, S. (2014, December 3). *Can you repair a relationship after an affair?* [Video]. YouTube. https://www.youtube.com/watch?v=G1Uy7YWdtwY

Killian, K. D. (2019, December 27). Sexual desire discrepancy: Why it's a big deal for couples. *Psychology Today.* https://www.psychologytoday.com/intl/blog/intersections/201912/sexual-desire-discrepancy-why-it-s-big-deal-couples

Kleine, M. (2019). Accounts and attributions following marital infidelity. *Western Journal of Communication, 85*(2), 211–229. https://doi.org/10.1080/10570314.2019.1702714

Labrecque, L. T. & Whisman, M. A. (2020). Extramarital sex and marital dissolution: Does identity of the extramarital partner matter? *Family Process, 59*(3), 1308–1318. https://doi.org/10.1111/famp.12472

Leeker O. & Carlozzi A. (2014). Effects of sex, sexual orientation, infidelity expectations, and love on distress related to emotional and sexual infidelity. *Journal of Marital and Family Therapy, 40*(1), 68–91. https://doi.org/10.1111/j.1752-0606.2012.00331.x

Lewandowski, G. (2021, May 21). Why do people in relationships cheat? *Scientific American.* https://www.scientificamerican.com/article/why-do-people-in-relationships-cheat/

Lusterman, D. (2008). Marital infidelity: The effects of delayed traumatic reaction. *Journal of Couple and Relationship Therapy, 4*(2–3), 71–81. https://doi.org/10.1300/J398v04n02_07

Mark, K., Janssen, E., & Milhausen, R. (2011). Infidelity in heterosexual couples: Demographic, interpersonal, and personality-related predictors of extradyadic sex. *Archives of Sexual Behavior, 40*(5), 971–982. https://doi.org/10.1007/s10508-011-9771-z

Marnie and Duane (Hosts). (2021, March 5). 27: PACT therapy, attachment and betrayal trauma with Stan Tatkin (no. 27) [Audio podcast episode]. *Helping Couples Heal.* https://redcircle.com/show/81e6d1e6-d3cb-456e-bf1e-1ffede344e6b/ep/b77ed01e-4562-423e-accd-a7b0b54e4f18

Mcintyre, J., Barlow, F., & Hayward, L. (2015). Stronger sexual desires only predict bold romantic intentions and reported infidelity when self-control is low. *Australian Journal of Psychology, (67)*3, 178–186. https://doi.org/10.1111/ajpy.12073

Mineo, Liz. (2017, April 11). Good genes are nice, but joy is better. *The Harvard Gazette.* https://news.harvard.edu/gazette/story/2017/04/over-nearly-80-years-harvard-study-has-been-showing-how-to-live-a-healthy-and-happy-life/

Moore, M. (2021, October 29). Long-term psychological effects of infidelity. *PsychCentral.* https://psychcentral.com/health/long-term-psychological-effects-of-infidelity

Morton, K. (n.d.). The 4 main attachment styles in relationships (and the attachment theory). [Video]. *YouTube.* https://www.youtube.com/watch?v=pL1NBH7LrXk

Pazhoohi, F. (2022). Cultural differences and similarities in the nature of infidelity. In T. DeLecce and T. K. Shackelford

(Eds.), *The Oxford Handbook of Infidelity.* https://doi.org/10.1093/oxfordhb/9780197502891.013.28

Perel, E. (2007). *Mating in captivity: Unlocking erotic intelligence.* Yellow Kite.

Perel, E. (2010). After the storm. *Psychotherapy Networker, 34*(4), 29–33.

Perel, E. (2017). *The state of affairs: Rethinking infidelity.* Harper Collins.

Perel, E. & Real, T. (2023). Esther Perel: "The state of Affairs" [Webinar]. *Relational Life Institute.* https://learn.relationallife.com/lessons/esther-perel-the-state-of-affairs-talk/

Phillips, L. (2020, April). Recovering from the trauma of infidelity. *Counseling Today.* https://ct.counseling.org/2020/04/recovering-from-the-trauma-of-infidelity/

Pollock, K. (2018, March). Social isolation and loneliness — The realities of modern life (and what we can do to change that). *AgeWise King County.* https://www.agewisekingcounty.org/ill_pubs_articles/social-isolation-loneliness-realities-modern-life-can-change/

Real, T. (2007). *The new rules of marriage. What you need to do to make love work.* Ballantine Books.

Real, T. (2016). Coming back from infidelity — A relational life approach [Webinar]. *Relational Life Institute.* https://learn.relationallife.com/lessons/3-coming-back-from-infidelity-a-relational-life-approach/

Real, T. (2017, November 14). Working with men, live Q&A call with Terry Real [Transcript]. *Relational Life Institute.*

Real, T. (2018, April 24). Multi-generational trauma: Healing the past to heal the present. Call two: The forging of the adaptive child [transcript]. *Relational life institute.*

Real, T. (2019). Love, sex, and power — Module 3: Sexual betrayal: Coming back from infidelity [Webinar]. *Relational Life*

Institute. https://learn.relationallife.com/lessons/module-3-sexual-betrayal-coming-back-from-infidelity/

Real, T. (2021). Staying in love: The art of fierce intimacy — The essential rhythm of relationships [Webinar]. *Relational Life Institute.* https://learn.relationallife.com/lessons/5-the-essential-rhythm-of-relationships/

Real, T. (2022, July 27). The level 3 RLT training course live class with Terry Real [Transcript]. *Relational Life Institute.*

Real, T. (2022a). *Us: Getting past you and me to build a more loving relationship.* Rodale Books.

Real, T. (2022b). Level 1, module 1: Introduction to Relational Life Therapy [Webinar]. *Relational Life Institute.* https://learn.relationallife.com/lessons/module-1-introduction-to-relational-life-therapy-3/

Real, T. (2022c). Level 1, module 2: Relational mindfulness — The two consciousnesses [Webinar]. *Relational Life Institute.* https://learn.relationallife.com/lessons/module-2-relational-mindfullness-the-two-consciousnesses/

Real, T. (2022d). Level 1, module 3: Data gathering — The seven lenses (1–4) [Webinar]. *Relational Life Institute.* https://learn.relationallife.com/lessons/module-3-data-gathering-the-seven-lenses-1-4/

Real, T. (2022e). Level 1, module 4: Data gathering — The seven lenses (5–7) [Webinar]. *Relational Life Institute.* https://learn.relationallife.com/lessons/module-4-data-gathering-the-seven-lenses-5-4/

Real, T. (2022f). Level 1, module 5: Finding leverage — Grandiosity as a demotivating force [Webinar]. *Relational Life Institute.* https://learn.relationallife.com/lessons/module-5-finding-leverage-grandiosity-as-a-demotivating-force/

Real, T. (2022g). Level 2, module 1: Reviewing latents and blatants [Webinar]. *Relational Life Institute.* https://learn.

relationallife.com/lessons/module-1-reviewing-blatants-and-latents-3/

Real, T. (2022h). Level 2, module 2: Moving from the present to each partner's family of origin [Webinar]. *Relational Life Institute.* https://learn.relationallife.com/lessons/module-2-moving-from-the-present-to-each-partners-family-of-origin/

Real, T. (2022i). Level 2, module 3: Working with deep trauma in the presence of one another [Webinar]. https://learn.relationallife.com/lessons/module-3-working-with-deep-trauma-in-the-presence-of-one-another/

Real, T. (2022j). Level 2, module 4: Dealing with resistance and amplifying progress [Webinar]. *Relational Life Institute.* https://learn.relationallife.com/lessons/module-4-dealing-with-resistance-and-amplifying-progress/

Real, T. (2022k). Level 2, module 5: Looking at attachment styles [Webinar]. *Relational Life Institute.* https://learn.relationallife.com/lessons/module-5-looking-at-attachment-styles/

Real, T. (2022l). RLT's approach to trauma work [Webinar]. *Relational Life Institute.* https://learn.relationallife.com/courses/rlts-approach-to-trauma-work/

Real, T. (2022m). Level 3, module 1: The RLT ecological perspective [Webinar]. *Relational Life Institute.* https://learn.relationallife.com/lessons/module-1-the-rlt-ecological-perspective/

Real, T. (2022n). Level 3, module 3: Family of origin work [Webinar]. *Relational Life Institute.* https://learn.relationallife.com/lessons/module-3-family-of-origin-work/

Real, T. (2022o). Level 3, module 4: The third phase of RLT [Webinar]. *Relational Life Institute.* https://learn.relationallife.com/lessons/module-4-the-third-phase-of-rlt/

Real, T. (2023, March 8). Working with infidelity class 3 [Transcript]. *Relational Life Institute.*

Real, T. (2023, July 6). Level 1 live class, July 6, 2023 [Transcript]. *Relational Life Institute.*

Real, T. (2023a). Class 1: An overview of the RLT approach to infidelity [Webinar]. *Relational Life Institute.* https://learn.relationallife.com/lessons/class-1-an-overview-of-the-rlt-approach-to-infidelity/

Real, T. (2023b). Class 2: The hurt partner: Infidelity as trauma [Webinar]. *Relational Life Institute.* https://learn.relationallife.com/lessons/class-2-the-hurt-partner-infidelity-as-a-trauma/

Real, T. (2023c). Class 3: The involved partner: Understanding the lack of "no" [Webinar]. *Relational Life Institute.* https://learn.relationallife.com/lessons/class-3-the-involved-partner-understanding-the-lack-of-no/

Real, T. (2023d). Class 4: Infidelity as an opportunity for transformation [Webinar]. *Relational Life Institute.* https://learn.relationallife.com/lessons/class-4-infidelity-as-an-opportunity-for-transformation/

Real, T. (2023e). Class 5: The crisis is over, now what? [Webinar]. *Relational Life Institute.* https://learn.relationallife.com/lessons/class-5-the-crisis-is-over-now-what/

Real, T. (n.d.) Multigenerational trauma [Webinar]. *Relational Life Institute.* https://learn.relationallife.com/courses/multigenerational-trauma/

Real, T. (n.d.-a). Working with infidelity: Disc one [Audio disc]. *Relational Life Institute.* https://learn.relationallife.com/lessons/disc-one-audio-download/

Real, T. (n.d.-b). Working with infidelity: Disc two [Audio disc]. *Relational Life Institute.* https://learn.relationallife.com/lessons/disc-two-audio-download/

Real, T. (n.d.-c). Working with infidelity: Disc three [Audio disc]. *Relational Life Institute.* https://learn.relationallife.com/lessons/disc-three-audio-download/

Real, T. (n.d.-d). Working with infidelity: Disc four [Audio disc]. *Relational Life Institute.* https://learn.relationallife.com/lessons/disc-four-audio-download/

Rokach, A. & Chan, S. (2023). Love and infidelity: Causes and consequences. *International Journal of Environmental Research and Public Health, 20*(5), 3904. doi: 10.3390/ijerph20053904

Schecter, T. & Gould, M. (2020). *Lead from your heart: The art of relationship-based leadership.* Iguana Books.

Scheeren, P., Alda Martinez de Apellaniz, I., & Wagner, A. (2018). Marital infidelity: The experience of men and women. *Trends in Psychology, 26*(1), 371–385. doi: 10.9788/TP2018.1-14En

Schonian, S. (2013). Perceptions and definition of infidelity: A multimethod study. *UNLV Theses, Dissertations, Professional Papers, and Capstones.* http://dx.doi.org/10.34917/5363941

Selterman, D., Garcia, J., & Tsapelas, I. (2021) What do people do, say, and feel when they have affairs? Associations between extradyadic infidelity motives with behavioral, emotional, and sexual outcomes. *Journal of Sex and Marital Therapy, 47*(3), 238–252. doi: 10.1080/0092623X.2020.1856987

Seltzer, L. (2019, April 17) Spouse had an affair? Beware how you handle your anger. *Psychology Today.* https://www.psychologytoday.com/us/blog/evolution-the-self/201904/spouse-had-affair-beware-how-you-handle-your-anger

Shore, J. & Real, T. (2020, October 15). The relational brain with Terry Real and Juliane Shore: Working with your client's brain in two different ways session 2 [Transcript]. *Relational Life Institute.*

Shore, J. & Real, T. (2020, November 5). The relational brain with Terry Real and Juliane Shore: Empathy, accountability, and vulnerability session 5 [Transcript]. *Relational Life Institute.*

Shore, J. & Real, T. (2022). The relational brain [Webinar]. *Relational Life Institute.* https://learn.relationallife.com/courses/the-relational-brain-2022/

Smith Investigation Agency. (2023). Infidelity statistics: Who cheats more men or women? https://smithinvestigationagency.com/blog/2023-infidelity-statistics-who-cheats-more-men-or-women/#:~:text=According%20to%20recent%20data%20gathered,in%20the%20last%2020%20years.

Tatkin, S. (2010). Infidelity, repairs, and reparation: A psychobiological approach to couple therapy. *New Therapist, 69*, 12–18.

Tatkin, S. (2011). *Wired for love.* New Harbinger Publications, Inc.

Tatkin, S. (2018). *We do: Saying yes to a relationship of depth, true connection, and enduring love.* Sounds True.

Tee-Melegrito, R. (2023, April 27). What to know about mismatched sex drives. *Medical News Today.* https://www.medicalnewstoday.com/articles/mismatched-sex-drives

UCLA Health. (2019, July 24). Study finds cultural differences in attitudes towards infidelity, jealousy. *UCLA Health.* https://www.uclahealth.org/news/study-finds-cultural-differences-in-attitudes-toward-infidelity-jealousy

Waldinger, R. (2016, January 25). What makes a good life? Lessons from the longest study on happiness [Video]. YouTube. https://www.youtube.com/watch?v=8KkKuTCFvzI&t=766s

Wang, W. (2018, January 10). Who cheats more? The demographics of infidelity in America [Blogpost]. *Institute for Family Studies.* https://ifstudies.org/blog/who-cheats-more-the-demographics-of-cheating-in-america#:~:text=Some%2022%25%20of%20ever%2Dmarried,and%2016%25%20of%20Hispanic%20men

Weiser, D. A., Lalasz, C. B., Weigel, D. J., Evans, W. P. (2014, November 4). A prototype analysis of infidelity. *Personal Relationships, 21*(4), 655–675. doi: 10.1111/pere.12056

Witcomb, G. (2016, April 21). How your income affects your partner's infidelity. *The Sydney Morning Herald.* https://www.smh.com.au/money/how-your-income-affects-your-partners-fidelity-20160421-goc3b7.html#

Acknowledgments

Bringing this book to life was a circuitous and unforeseen journey. Throughout it, the one constant was people's input; without it, this book would be less engaging, more verbose, and far less useful. To each of these people, I owe a debt of gratitude. Specifically, Bruce Hardy, one of my first readers, was a great sounding board. He allowed me to talk through my ideas, provided encouragement, asked thoughtful questions, and offered many gentle suggestions, all of which helped me create my first draft and made it infinitely better.

Alan Stamp, a very early reader, provided me, along with a much-needed dose of cheerleading, extremely valuable feedback that allowed me to fine-tune the book's last chapter. Tiffany Wainwright then helped identify the missing ingredient that made this chapter complete.

Nicole Nosiak generously provided me with many editorial suggestions on an early draft while asking pointed questions. Together, these helped clarify my thoughts and made me better able to convey them in a clearer form. Tzippy Corber, my mother, provided a deep dive edit on the final manuscript. Her insightful edits — all of which she made as a labor of love in her spare time as she entered her 80th year — helped make this book more succinct, on point, and coherent.

Greg Ioannou, editor extraordinaire, graciously coached and encouraged me through the final stretch. He spent hours with me on Zoom calls, pointing out areas where my manuscript could be refined while helping me smooth out its rough edges so that my voice could shine through. Thanks also to Amanda Feeney, who was a pleasure to work with as she applied her precision editorial skills to the final manuscript in a way that made the final copy clearer, crisper, and error-free.

Thanks to Cheryl Hawley for her patience in answering all my questions related to the process of bring a book to life, her help in doing so, and for her skills in laying this book out so that it feels like a pleasure to read.

And, last but not least, thank you to Jennifer Papineau, my long-time visual collaborator, who not only created the beautiful graphic for the CHI Relationship Map, but also designed this book's appealing and on-point cover.

Of course, no book is ever written without those who quietly support writers from the wings. In this case, it's my husband, Olivier Grard. Not only did he provide me with encouragement and unwavering belief in my ability to write this book, he also picked up the slack in our lives on the many afternoons I spent holed up in my office with my computer. Although I am the author, this book could not have existed without all of these people who supported me and were personally invested in both the process and its outcome. Thank you.

www.ingramcontent.com/pod-product-compliance
Lightning Source LLC
Chambersburg PA
CBHW031207270326
41931CB00006B/447